CHRISTIAN: TAKE HEART!

CHRISTIAN: TAKE HEART!

*Truth About the Christian Life
and its Progress*

TOM WELLS

THE BANNER OF TRUTH TRUST

137573

THE BANNER OF TRUTH TRUST
3 Murrayfield Road, Edinburgh, EH12 6EL
PO Box 621, Carlisle, Pennsylvania 17013, USA

★

© Tom Wells 1987
First published 1987
ISBN 0 85151 508 8

★

Set in 10½/12pt Linotron Plantin
Typeset at The Spartan Press Ltd,
Lymington, Hants
and printed and bound in Great Britain by
Hazell Watson & Viney Limited,
Member of the BPCC Group,
Aylesbury, Bucks

★

Contents

With special recognition to my wife,
LUANN WELLS,
who daily exemplifies the truth about the Christian
life which I have tried to explain in the pages of this book.

1: *Robbing God's People*

Do you remember a piece of poetry by Gelett Burgess, entitled *The Purple Cow*? Here it is:

> *I've never seen a Purple Cow,*
> *I never hope to see one;*
> *But I can tell you, anyhow,*
> *I'd rather see than be one.*

The Pharisee in the Lord's story of the Pharisee and the Publican had seen many things about which he could say: 'I'd rather see than be one!' He named them over. 'God', he said, 'I've seen adulterers. I've seen unjust men. I've seen thieves. I'm only glad, God, that I've just seen such people. I'm so glad, God, that I'm not a thief!'

The Pharisee would have seen himself differently if he had used God's Word for his mirror. Many of our judgments about ourselves are like the funhouse mirrors that make us look tall and straight when we are not. The Lord has put it this way: 'All a man's ways seem right to him, but the Lord weighs the heart' (*Proverbs 21:2*). We readily deceive ourselves. We pull the wool over our own eyes.

In a way, this book is a confession. I too have been a thief. I have stolen God's Word from His people. I did not do it as blatantly as those that we used to call 'the liberals'. No, my own way was much more subtle. When I looked at the liberals I said: 'I'd rather see than be one.'

But I also robbed God's people. Not in a wholesale way,

but piecemeal. I, and others who thought like me, robbed God's people of one class of promises. It seems characteristic of much preaching today, even by godly men, to rob God's people in this way. Of course that does not excuse me. I mention others for this reason: many of you who read this are teachers in one way or another. You are preachers, or Sunday School teachers, or parents. Consider carefully what I write. I hope to help you as I have been helped.

I find in God's Word a number of statements about Christians that seem too good to be true. Let me give you some examples. After each example I want to show you how many of us who teach have tended to explain them.

Let us look first at John 7:38. Here are Jesus' words: 'Whoever believes in me, as the Scripture has said, streams of living water will flow from within him.' The writer, John, adds in the next verse: 'By this he meant the Spirit, whom those who believed in him were later to receive.'

What do these verses mean? At one time I think I would have said something like this: 'If you're a Christian God wants the Holy Spirit to flow out of you in life-giving power.' There is something radically wrong with that understanding of these verses, but it took me a long time to see it. Do you see it? Before I tell you what I think the problem is, let's look at another verse.

My next example is Romans 6:14. Paul told the Roman believers: 'Sin shall not be your master . . .' That means, I once would have said, that you must not let sin get dominion over you! What is wrong with that explanation? Much!

Let me quote one more verse, Romans 8:14. 'Those who are led by the Spirit of God are sons of God.' What does that mean? Many would say: 'God wants to lead you, Christian, by His Spirit, if you will only let Him!' What is wrong with that understanding of this verse? Everything!

The verses you have just read all have one thing in common. They are plain statements of fact about believers. Look at them again. 'Whoever believes in me,' Jesus said, '. . . streams of living water will flow from within him.' That, you see, is a glorious statement of fact. If a man is a believer in Christ that promise is true of him. He may – and he must – ask what that means. But whatever it may mean it is a distortion to say, 'This is what God hopes to do, or wants to do, in every believer.' John 7.38 says nothing about what God *wants* to do. Not a word! But it does something else. It says a great deal about what God *actually does* in every believer. The Holy Spirit comes to live in, and in varying degrees to flow out of, every believer. *Every believer without exception!* That is just as true of one believer as of another. Every believer has this river within him and flowing out of him. What right, then, had I to say that this was true of some believers, but not of others?

Let us look at Romans 6:14 again. This verse is in a passage about the Christian's fight against sin. Paul has a real struggle in view, one that goes on throughout the believer's life. But Paul's cry is triumphant: 'Sin shall not be your master . . . !' That is a clear statement of fact, a fact that excites Paul deeply. What right does any man have to change Paul's 'shall not' into 'should not'? Didn't Paul write by inspiration of God? When God says 'shall not' we may be sure that He knows what He means.

Again, Romans 8:14 says clearly: 'Those who are led by the Spirit of God are sons of God.' This verse says nothing about a select group of believers who are more spiritual or more holy than other Christians. Not at all! It simply equates two groups, those who are led by the Spirit, and those who are God's sons. Every one led by the Spirit is a son. Every one who is a son is led by the Spirit. If you are a

son of God, Spirit-leadership is a fact in your life. That is
what Paul says. What right has any man to say something
else?

We have looked at three verses often misused in this
way. There are many others. I am talking about straightforward statements of fact that are turned into wishes or
desires on God's part. A verse may tell us what God has
determined to do, but we are not content to leave it at that.
We insist on making it speak of what God *wants* to do.
Certainly He *wants* to! No one forces Him to do what He
does. God is free to do as He pleases. But that does not
allow us to cast doubt on plain statements of fact. Do we
suppose that the Lord may be thwarted in what He sets
out to do?

Let me give you one more example of what I am talking
about. At a Bible conference at which I was speaking some
years ago I heard another speaker quote 2 Corinthians
5:17. That verse says, 'If anyone is in Christ, he is a new
creation.' Then the speaker added: 'God wants to make
you a new creature!' Wants to!? Thank God, that verse
says nothing about what God *wants* to do. A Christian – if
he is a Christian at all – *is* a new creation! That is a simple
and glorious statement of fact.

This kind of statement reveals a frame of mind that is
widespread among Christian teachers. In a nutshell it
might be put this way: God is *not* at work in His people!
No one that I know of would defend that statement when
it is put so baldly. I understand that. But as a general
attitude toward believers I see it everywhere. I hear it in
words like these: 'The trouble with Christians is that they
are so undedicated.' Or these: 'If we didn't have so many
worldly Christians we could get a job done for God.' Or
simply: 'The average Christian is carnal.' Of course, if a
Christian worker really believes these things he must
address himself to them. God help him if he does not!

But are they true? Is the average Christian really carnal? Is sin his master? Do not streams of living water flow out of him, as God has said? Do not God's plain statements of fact mean what they say? If they do – as every Christian must believe – have we not been guilty of putting an 'if' where God has put an exclamation point? These are the questions we must face.

In the rest of this book I will discuss these questions. I will try to show you that God is very much at work in each of His people. I will try to show that the sweeping statements above about the state of Christians are not true. I think I can show you from the Bible that you have every reason to be encouraged if you are a believer in Jesus Christ. I believe I will be able to say to some of God's dear saints, 'Christian, take heart!'

Before I close this chapter let me say a word about the men (including myself) who have taught that Christians are usually carnal. I do not doubt these men's motives. For the most part they are good motives. This is not an attack on godly men. I see at least four reasons why good men have been afraid to say, 'God is at work in each of His people.' In addition I think I see one other reason which is wrong, though common. Here are the five reasons, along with why I think them mistaken.

First, we have been much too quick, I believe, to think that we know who is a Christian and who is not. I will say much about this in the course of this book, so I do not want to labour it now. But think about it for a moment. It must be clear that if I take a man to be a believer and he frequently acts in an ungodly way, that fact in itself will decide what I think a Christian can or cannot be like.

Second, there is much in our experience of ourselves and of other Christians which seems to contradict the fact that God is at work in each of His own, in each believer. I will try to show you that experience alone is not a good measure of how spiritual we are. We will touch upon this theme again and again. The truth that I will contend for is this: we must always judge our experience by the Word of God. We must never make God's Word conform to our experience. Some day, in eternity, we shall have our eyes opened. Then we shall see that what we experienced exactly matched what God said. There can be no contradiction. God is God in every sphere. His Word and His work agree.

Until we enter the eternal state we are certain to be tempted to doubt God's Word because of our ignorance. We cannot see how it matches what happens in us and to us. With the Lord's help I hope to show you that you do not need to deny your experience to know that God is at work in each believer.

There is a third reason why some of us have not often said: 'God is at work in you who believe.' We have feared to make Christians self-satisfied. We have been afraid of what Christians might do if they heard those encouraging words. Perhaps they would congratulate themselves. Like Little Jack Horner they might sit in a corner and say, 'What a good boy am I!' That is a disgusting prospect!

God, however, is much more interested in saving His people from self-satisfaction than we are. He has made provision against just this error. If you think about it you will realise that the balance of truth is the thing most likely to keep all of us from distorting the facts about the Christian life. There is no need to neglect the cheering truths in order to keep Christians straight. Every word from God is profitable. We must never forget that.

There is a fourth reason why we have hesitated to say: 'God is at work in each of His people.' There are a number of passages in God's Word that might suggest the opposite! In the Old Testament especially there are repeated warnings against backsliding. Nor is that all!

The New Testament urgently calls upon Christians to forsake all sin, lest we pay the consequence of lost rewards or loss of soul. We dare not trifle with such words. We must face them for what they say. We dare not minimise them.

In a general way I will say now that many of these texts that appear applicable to Christians at first glance, do not prove to be so on a closer look. Each Bible verse is directed to some one or some class in particular. If we apply texts intended for unbelievers to Christians we may misuse God's Word. We must not do that. We resent it when unbelievers take the promises that belong to Christians and apply them to men at large. We must not do the opposite.

And here is one more thing to reckon with. Some things may be true of a Christian at a given moment in his life, that could never be characteristic of his life as a whole. Think about that! That may be the most important thing you learn from this book, if you are truly a believer. *The Christian life is a life characterised by righteousness and marred by sin.* If we do not see the difference between what is *habitually* true of a man and what is *occasionally* true of him, we miss a great distinction. And a biblical one!

There is one final reason why, in the past, we have avoided telling God's people that God is actively at work in them. This reason is not as commendable as the others. But it is very common. I fear that I, and others like me, have wanted to put all God's people in one mould. Their individuality threatened us. We insisted that they all be alike. When they resisted, we concluded that they were carnal. What is worse, they believed us! Is it any wonder that they felt defeated?

Suppose that I insist that you do something or be something that God never intended you to do or to be. Or suppose I over-emphasise some good thing that God commands. If you do not follow me in my over-emphasis or error what will happen? Very likely you will feel guilty. You will be defeated. On the other hand, suppose you do follow me. Suppose you try to be what I want you to be. If God is not at work in you to make you that kind of person you will constantly be tense. You will not be able to keep up. Once again defeat will come.

That is a hard lesson for teachers and preachers to learn. If we set up standards that God never set up for His people we need not be surprised if they do not follow us. They may be worse off if they try. We may pick on something easy for us to do. We may insist that other Christians conform. But if the Lord is not at work to help them they will probably fall. Or, if they succeed, they may do it with the kind of pride that Paul calls 'self-imposed worship' (*Colossians 2:23*). They may feel superior to God's other people. We might as well call such feelings what they are – sin! Is it any wonder that James said: 'Not many of you should presume to be teachers, my brothers, because you know that we who teach will be judged more strictly' (*James 3:1*)? May the Lord help all of us who teach others! May he grant that we will be faithful to His word!

2: What is a Carnal Christian?

It is hard to trace an idea to its source. The notion that many Christians are not spiritual, but carnal or worldly, may go back many years. I do not know. I do know this, however. The assertion that many Christians are carnal is often associated with a single note in the old Scofield Bible. That note is a footnote to I Corinthians 2:14. It says in part, 'Paul divides men into three classes.' Dr Scofield then lists these classes as he understands them. He speaks of a natural man, that is a man unrenewed by the Spirit, what we commonly call an 'unsaved man.'

Dr Scofield goes on to divide Christians into two classes. First, a spiritual man, 'i.e. the renewed man as Spirit-filled and walking in the Spirit in full communion with God (*Eph. 5:18–20*) . . .' He then speaks of a carnal or fleshly man, 'i.e. the renewed man who, walking "after the flesh," remains a babe in Christ (*I Cor. 3:1–4*).'

Dr Scofield's note has been taken to mean a good deal more than Paul would have allowed. First, it has suggested to many that a man may remain 'a babe in Christ' indefinitely. Strictly speaking, Paul does not say that, and for all I know C. I. Scofield did not mean to imply it. But 'remains' has an ominous sound about it when it is used without any limits.

Here are Paul's words in the passage (*I Corinthians 3:1–4*):

Brothers, I could not address you as spiritual but as worldly – mere infants in Christ. I gave you milk, not solid food, for you were not yet ready for it. Indeed, you are still not ready. You are still worldly. For since there is jealousy and quarrelling among you, are you not worldly? Are you not acting like mere men? For when one says, 'I follow Paul,' and another, 'I follow Apollos,' are you not mere men?

(Note that the NIV, which I am quoting, uses the words 'worldly' and 'infants' where Dr Scofield's note, based on the King James Version, has 'carnal' and 'babes'.)

At first glance it might appear that Paul does indeed wish us to understand that the Corinthian Christians were not spiritual men, but worldly men. His question, 'Are you not worldly?' is intended to receive an affirmative answer. The Corinthians were supposed to say, 'Yes, we are worldly men. Paul has said so, and we must admit that he is right.' It seems that this is spoken about as plainly as a man can speak.

But we have good reason not to understand Paul in this way. And the reason is found in the passage itself.

Do you remember the difference between a *metaphor* and a *simile*? The dictionary on my desk gives these definitions:

Simile: a figure of speech in which one thing is likened to another, dissimilar thing by the use of *like*, *as*, etc. (e.g., a heart as big as a whale, her tears flowed like wine): distinguished from *metaphor*, in that the comparison is made explicit.
Metaphor: a figure of speech in which one thing is likened to another, different thing by being spoken of as if it were that other; implied comparison, in which a word or phrase ordinarily and primarily used of one thing is applied to another (e.g., screaming headlines, 'all the world's a stage').

The quickest way to see how Paul is using his language

here is to put what he says about the Corinthians in two columns, as follows:

EXPRESSED COMPARISONS (SIMILES)	PLAIN STATEMENTS (METAPHORS)
'as worldly' (*v. 1*)	'worldly' (*v. 3*)
'as infants' (*v. 1*)	(see discussion)
'like mere men' (*v. 3*)	'mere men' (*v. 4*)

Look first at the left column. Here we clearly have *similes*. The Corinthians are 'like' this or that group of people. Now look across at the right column. The words 'like' and 'as' are missing. Paul has dropped his *similes* there, and turned them into *metaphors*. In other words, he is now calling the Corinthians the very kinds of people that he compared them to, moments before. Earlier they were like worldly men; now they *are* worldly. But what is Paul doing? I hope to show you in a moment, but first I need to say a word about the text I have used in the columns above.

Note that I have supplied the word 'as' before the word 'infants' in the left-hand column. The Greek text has it. Our translators did not repeat it a second time to smooth out the English. Notice too that Paul does not call the Corinthians 'infants' in a later verse. It is clear, however, that that is his meaning in verse 2 when he says, 'You still are not ready [for solid food].' That is another way of saying, 'You are infants.' All told, then, Paul has three *similes* that he turns into three *metaphors*.

But are we really dealing with figures of speech here. Let's see. In verse 4 Paul asks, 'Are you not mere men?' What can that mean? Is Paul asking whether the Corinthians were human beings? Surely not! That would be a truism. No one ever doubted that the men and women of Corinth were members of the human race. No, a 'mere man' here would be a natural man, a man unrenewed by the Spirit of God.

Paul was asking these Corinthians, 'Are you not mere unregenerate men?' And his question expects the answer, 'Yes, we are!' Paul is calling these men and women something far worse than immature believers. He is calling them ungodly! To say that they are worldly or carnal or mere men is to say that they are unsaved.

'But wait a minute,' I hear you say. 'Paul is writing to "brothers" (v. 1)! Surely he is addressing Christians and not mere worldlings. Can't you see that?' And I am not surprised at the impatience in your voice, for of course you are right!

Paul was writing to Christians, to 'saints' (1:2). That lies on the face of the letter. There may have been unconverted men among the Corinthians, but Paul was not singling them out. He was speaking to the same people that he had called 'infants in Christ', that is, he was speaking to believers. Yet he called them 'mere men.' He could not have been speaking literally, then. He was using a metaphor, a figure of speech. In verse 3 he used a simile when he asked, 'Are you not acting like mere men?' In verse 4 he dropped the expressed comparison. Instead he implied it in asking, 'Are you not mere men?'

We must not be surprised to find Paul using metaphors. He has the example of the Lord Jesus Himself. You will remember Jesus' statement to Peter, 'Out of my sight, Satan!' (*Matthew 16:23*). Surely Peter was not Satan! But when he was like Satan (simile), Jesus did not hesitate to use the bold figure. Paul, by inspiration, was prepared to speak in the same graphic way.

Were the Corinthians 'worldly' or 'carnal'? Not if we take those words in their straightforward literal sense. A worldly man, or a carnal man, is an unregenerate man. That is why Paul says elsewhere, 'If you live according to the sinful nature [Greek – *carnally*], you will die', and

'Those controlled by the sinful nature [Greek – *Those who are carnal*] cannot please God' (*Romans 8:13,8*). A man who cannot please God is a faithless man (*Hebrews 11:6*). Such a man is lost. If he does not change he will remain lost for ever.

We see, then, Paul's meaning in this passage. Without denying that there may have been both carnal men and babes in Christ in the Corinthian church, Paul was not speaking to those select groups. No, he was characterising the entire church as 'worldly', 'infants', and as 'mere men'. But he adopted these figures of speech to let them know how much he abhorred their attitudes. Little could he have guessed that later in history men would take these figures literally to divide the people of God into two distinct types.

Whatever merit or demerit there may be in such a division, it cannot be made to rest on this text. Paul no more taught us to believe that some Christians are really 'carnal' than Christ taught us that some Christians are 'Satan'. In each case the sharp language is intended to rebuke a particularly repugnant attitude. Nothing more than that should be read into the text.

Every parent with older children will know what I mean. I may say to one of my girls, 'Do you want me to act as if you are not my child? Or do you want me to treat you like an infant, like a baby?' She knows what I mean. I mean that in one area of her life, or at one point in time, she is not acting like my grown-up daughter. I do not mean to imply that she will stay that way all her life. Far from it! She has grown. I expect her to keep growing. I also think that speaking to her in this way will help to pull her out of the habit or mood to which I object.

Some have taken Dr Scofield's note to mean that a Christian may keep walking 'after the flesh' both char-acteristically and indefinitely. If that were true it would not be surprising if the average Christian in our day were carnal. If left to ourselves we no doubt would sink to a low level and stay there. Thank God, however, we are not left to ourselves! The Bible plainly teaches that God works in His people to keep them from *habitually* walking apart from Him. In a believer, a carnal or fleshly walk can only be temporary and partial. There is no such thing as a *characteristically* carnal Christian. That would be a contradiction in terms. As Paul said elsewhere,

> The mind of sinful man is death, but the mind controlled by the Spirit is life and peace. (*Romans 8:6*)

But the Christian has new life, eternal life in Christ. His life is the very opposite of the deadly mind of the unconverted man.

I do not expect you to take my word for this. The first Epistle of John is largely devoted to this subject. Let us see what God has said through John:

> We know that we have come to know him if we obey his commands. The man who says, 'I know him,' but does not do what he commands is a liar, and the truth is not in him. But if any one obeys his word, God's love is truly made complete in him. This is how we know we are in him. (*2:3–5*)

Note what John does here. He tells us that there are two kinds of men and women who profess to know Christ. First, those who claim to know Him and prove it by their obedience. Second, those who claim to know Him, but are liars. How does John know that they lie? They do not keep God's commands – that is how he knows!

These three verses do not stand alone in 1 John. Here are four more:

> Dear children, do not let anyone lead you astray. He who does what is right is righteous, just as he is

righteous. He who does what is sinful is of the devil, because the devil has been sinning from the beginning. The reason the Son of God appeared was to destroy the devil's work. No one who is born of God will continue in sin, because God's seed remains in him; he cannot go on sinning, because he has been born of God. This is how we know who the children of God are and who the children of the devil are: Anyone who does not do what is right is not a child of God; neither is anyone who does not love his brother. (*3:7–10*)

These are strong words indeed! Let us see what they mean.

John does not mean that a Christian cannot perform an act of sin. Earlier he has told us that Christians indeed do sinful acts. 'If we claim to be without sin, we deceive ourselves . . .'(*1:8*). No, he is not speaking of perfection. We must wait until we are in the presence of Christ to be utterly sinless.

John is talking about the habits of the Christian and the non-Christian. A man who is *habitually* sinful is not a Christian. A life that is *characteristically* disobedient is not from God. Christ came to destroy the works of the devil in a believer. For that reason a believer does what is right. That is John's position. He goes so far as to say that he can tell the children of the devil apart from the children of God by how they act.

There are, then, no Christians who walk 'after the flesh' characteristically. There are temporarily 'carnal' Christians. There are Christians who may repeatedly do some carnal deed or hold some worldly attitude. We cannot deny that. But John could not be plainer: there is no such thing as a habitually carnal Christian. Such a man is not even a poor Christian. He is not a Christian at all.

I need to add a few words of caution here. First, you must not suppose that any man is saved by his own righteousness. John does not mean that Christ receives men because they are good. Far from it! God saves the ungodly. 'I have not come to call the righteous,' Jesus said, 'but sinners' (*Mark 2:17*). That is clear enough, and thank God that it is so! There would have been no hope for you and me otherwise.

John means something quite different. The whole Bible bears witness to the point he is making. It is this. God does not merely save from hell, God saves from sin as well. We may put this another way. An obedient walk is not a cause of salvation, it is an effect of God's working in the soul. The *cause* of our salvation is God's mercy, God's grace. One *result* of our salvation – or, one part of our salvation – is our beginning to walk as God wants us to walk. We do not take our steps perfectly. We fail in some instances and in some circumstances. Far too many! But, if we are truly believers, our lives are characteristically right. However strange it may seem to us to say this, John insists that it is so. God is at work in each of His people to make them like His Son. What a wonderful fact! Christian, take heart!

Here is another word of caution. Do not think that John is anxious to see us scurrying around measuring others. That is the temptation, isn't it? John intends to encourage us with the work of God in our own souls, and to help us to measure ourselves. That should keep us busy. Remember Paul's question, 'Who are you to judge someone else's servant? To his own master he stands or falls' (*Romans 14:4*).

3: *What About Assurance?*

In the next chapter I want to return to this encouraging theme: God is at work in our lives. But just now I must step aside to meet an objection. It goes like this. 'If what you are saying is true, Tom, then how can any man be assured that he belongs to Christ? If our assurance depends on our performance, we shall always be riddled with doubts. What assurance is there in that? This is a question of enormous importance. I do not want to slight it in any way.

Let me start with a distinction. It is one thing to seek assurance. It is another thing to test assurance that we already have, to see if it is genuine. John nowhere teaches that we get our initial assurance from our works. On the contrary, he assumes that we already have assurance. You can see that by the way he writes. Listen to him again. 'If we claim to have fellowship with him . . .' Or, he speaks of the man 'who says, "I know him"' (*1 John 1:6; 2:4*). The man who claims fellowship with God and who says 'I know God' is not a man seeking assurance. He is a man who has assurance. There is a great difference here. Let me underline it to make myself understood. Once again: *it is one thing to seek assurance, and another thing to test it after I have it.* Please keep these distinctions in mind, or you will not be able to follow me further.

Let us talk a little about what assurance is. If we are confused about that we cannot go any further. We will need to see just what the Scripture says on this subject. A key passage is Romans 8:15–16:

> For you did not receive a spirit that makes you a slave again to fear, but you received the Spirit of sonship. And by him we cry, '*Abba*, Father.' The Spirit himself testifies with our spirit that we are God's children.

Let me point up several things here. First, Paul is clearly describing assurance as it exists in all God's children. This statement is not for some select few of His people. It belongs to every believer. Some Christians may have a more robust faith in their acceptance with God, a fuller assurance, but Paul is not speaking of them particularly. He includes them with all the rest of us who trust in Christ. We all cry, 'Father!' That is as true of one Christian as it is of another.

Second, Paul tells us that the inclination to call God 'Father' is the work of the Spirit. The Holy Spirit puts this in our hearts. He is 'the Spirit of sonship.' We would not be inclined to call God 'Father' if the Spirit did not move us to do so. This feeling of sonship that we have, this gift that moves us to look up to God as our Father, lies at the heart of biblical assurance. Nothing more than this is required for a man to have assurance. And nothing less than this will do.

Yet this idea – the view that the impulse to call God 'Father' is the heart of assurance – needs to be guarded carefully. We may misunderstand it in two ways.

First, we must be sure that we see this truth tied to all that has come before it in Romans. Paul has told us, for example, of the wickedness of the human heart. And he has included us all. He has omitted none of us. 'There is no one righteous, not even one' (*Romans 3:10*). *The mere inclination to call God 'Father', apart from a sense of my own deep sinfulness, is not the work of the Spirit of God.* Note this carefully. It is extremely important. Nothing is easier than to teach men to address God as 'Father'. But the Spirit's work is different in this way: the Spirit teaches men to call God 'Father', who would otherwise fear to do so because of what they know of their own sin.

The second danger we need to guard against is more subtle. When I say that the Spirit creates a feeling or sense of sonship in the believer that leads the Christian to call God 'Father', that is all I mean. I do *not* mean that the believer has necessarily drawn any inferences from his sense of sonship. If you ask him, for instance, 'Do you know where you would go if you died today?' he may not know the answer. It may seem obvious to us that he would go to be with the Lord. But that may not be clear to him at all. The Spirit of God has led him to call God 'Father', and he does so. Beyond that, however, he may not have drawn any conclusions. Even with our help he may find it difficult to do so.

Let me tell you why this point is important. If we overstate the content of the assurance that all Christians should have, then one of two things will happen. Either we will deny that all Christians have a measure of assurance, or we will refuse to accept others as genuine believers who do not measure up to our high standard. Yet Paul is plain. The Spirit works this work in all believers. None are excluded. Paul does not insist, however, on anything beyond this. A man may be a true believer, a genuine child of God, without drawing any further conclusions about what his sonship must imply. And, in fact, there seem to be many Christians of this kind.

If you have followed me thus far you will see why I have said that we do not get our assurance from our works. If a man has no assurance we must never send him to his own works. We must send him to Christ. Faith in the work of the Son of God is what he needs. When he turns to Christ the Spirit will give him the sense of sonship that I have been speaking of.

Hopefully, however, he will grow. The day should come – and come shortly, if all is well – when the professed believer will draw his conclusions. He will reflect on what God has done in him. If he suffered much fear before coming to Christ, he may be struck by a new-found relief. He will compare that with the Scriptures. And he will begin to say, 'I am in fellowship with God. I know Christ. I am confident that I am a Christian.' It is not certain that he will arrive at this point, but he should do so. *And when that hour comes it will be time to test his profession to see if it is genuine.*

Now I think I hear an objection forming in your mind. It goes something like this. 'If assurance is the work of God's Spirit why would it need to be tested?' That is an important question. Let me try to answer it.

At first glance it must seem needless, even arrogant, to check up on a man's or woman's assurance if it comes from God's Spirit. But I think I can show you why it has to be done. The reason is this: *psychologically all assurance is alike.* It makes no difference what its source is. The man who is sure, is sure, no matter how he became sure. Assurance is the state of mind of a person who is certain of some fact. Whether he has good grounds for his certainty is another question entirely. Think of the times we have all been sure of something that turned out to be a fallacy, a mistaken belief. So we must not only know that George Smith is sure that he is a Christian. We must also know that his certainty came from the Spirit of God. And how can we find that out? Or, more importantly, for this is the real point, how can George find that out? It is not usually *our* business to delve deeply into George's profession of faith, but it certainly is *his*. We can be certain that the Lord has not left George Smith to flounder over this question. No, a great deal in the New Testament speaks to it, and speaks to it directly.

The book of 1 John is an example. Throughout the book my profession of faith in Christ is weighed and tested. So also is George Smith's – and yours, *if* you have assurance that you belong to Christ!

How does John do this? In at least three ways. First he looks at our attitudes toward Jesus Christ. Listen to this:

> Who is the liar? It is the man who denies that Jesus is the Christ. Such a man is the antichrist – he denies the Father and the Son. No-one who denies the Son has the Father; whoever acknowledges the Son has the Father also. (*1 John 2:22–23*)

Here is a doctrinal test. A man is not free to hold whatever view he pleases about Jesus Christ and still be right with God. If a person claims to know God his claim is worthless unless he clings to the Bible's teaching about Jesus. As John asks later,

> Who is it that overcomes the world? Only he who believes that Jesus is the Son of God. (*5:5*)

'Experience' is not enough. Good feelings are not necessarily an accurate gauge of whether we are right with God. It is not enough to feel an inward glow. Our minds must have definite convictions about who Jesus is. That is John's first test.

Second, John checks our attitude towards other believers in Christ. He calls them our 'brothers'. And John tells us:

> Anyone who claims to be in the light but hates his brother is still in the darkness. Whoever loves his brother lives in the light, and there is nothing in him to make him stumble. But whoever hates his brother is in the darkness and walks around in the darkness; he does

not know where he is going, because the darkness has blinded him. (*2:9–11*)

Love for those who love Christ is an acid test. If we have this love we are 'in the light'. If we do not have it our profession means nothing. And let me add this. 'Love' here is not primarily a feeling. That is the way we usually think of love. In some contexts 'love' *is* a feeling, a passion. But that is not its only thrust in the New Testament. *To love someone, as John and others use the term, is to seek that person's benefit.* It means to be ready *and active* in helping others. We do not love our fellow Christians, or anyone else, when we merely feel warmth toward them. Not at all! We love them when we seek to do them good.

That brings us to John's third test. John tests our actions against the commands of Scripture. Do we claim to know God? Here are John's words to us:

> We know that we have come to know him if we obey his commands. The man who says, 'I know him,' but does not do what he commands is a liar, and the truth is not in him. But if anyone obeys his word, God's love is truly made complete in him. This is how we know we are in him: whoever claims to live in him must walk as Jesus did. (*1 John 2:3–6*)

These verses speak for themselves. We may think of the Old Testament as the book that majors on law, but the New Testament also has many commands to be obeyed. It is our duty to find these commands and to carry them out. It is true that we set out to keep them with assurance that God has *already received us* on the basis of Christ's merits, not on any supposed merits of our own. We must never fall into that trap. No, we are right with God only by His grace. Even so, God has changed us. That change is seen when we find a command of God. We seek to obey it. We address our minds to that command. We strive to carry it out.

[30]

I may say this in another way by reminding you that the Christian is a servant of Christ. To be sure, he is more than that. He is a son of God and God's heir. But that is not all. He is also Christ's servant. And a servant is a person who receives commands and carries them out.

Does that sound harsh? Just a moment ago I got up from my desk and took down from my bookshelf a Greek concordance. I opened it to look up a few verses that make the point that the Christian is the servant of Christ. But I was in for a mild surprise. Instead of the handful of examples I expected to see, I found dozens. Many are from the lips of the Lord Jesus Himself. Although I looked at the word for servant that also can mean slave (doulos), we may understand it in its broadest sense as servant. Either way the point is clear. A Christian is a man under orders. If he is not that, he is not a Christian!

I may put this yet another way. In recent years philosophers have been speaking about *self-involving language*. What they have said is this: some statements demand a response from the man who makes them. You cannot, for example, say that Jesus is Lord, and just leave it at that. No, if you say, 'Jesus is Lord', you must also say something else. You must also say, 'I am His slave.' There is no doubt that the Bible means to tell us the same thing. And it does so with the authority of God. But someone may say, 'It is all well and good to call believers "slaves", but in fact in writing to the Galatians Paul denies it point blank.' And at first glance the person who says this seems to be right. Let us look at Paul's words:

> Because you are sons, God sent the Spirit of his Son into our hearts, the Spirit who calls out, '*Abba*, Father.' So you are no longer a slave, but a son; and since you are a son, God has made you also an heir. (*Galatians 4:6–7*)

That is plain enough. 'You are no longer a slave, but a son.'

The key to Paul's meaning lies in the context. He has a certain kind of slavery in view. It is that special sort of slavery from which Christians have been delivered. Listen to him again:

> When we were children, we were in slavery under the basic principles of the world. [And again] . . . Formerly, when you did not know God, you were slaves to those who by nature are not gods. (*Galatians 4:3,8*)

The Christian is delivered from these slaveries once and for all! From these kinds of bondage, he is free. But we must not misunderstand his freedom. God has purchased the believer to be God's own servant. And the Christian is under orders to serve the God who saved him. He is in bondage to the One who said, 'My burden is light' (*Matthew 11:30*). He discovers the truth of John's words:

> This is love for God: to obey his commands. And his commands are not burdensome. (*1 John 5:3*)

And he takes to heart this word of Paul:

> You are not your own; you were bought at a price. Therefore honour God with your body. (*1 Corinthians 6:19–20*. Compare *7:22–23*)

Let me sum up. The gist of the matter is this: what I will call 'initial assurance' is common to all Christians. It is that sense of sonship to God that moves us to call Him 'Father'. This initial assurance may be all that some Christians have. Certainly it shows that God has saved them. But in another sense they ought to seek fuller assurance. Initial assurance, as the term implies, is only the beginning. There is much more to be had. It is reached by learning what is implied in sonship. It is increased mainly by the hearing and reading of God's Word.

When a man or woman gains confidence in his or her standing before God it is time to test assurance. At that point he must apply such tests as we have seen in 1 John. Does the person hold the biblical doctrine of Christ? Does he seek the benefit of fellow believers? Does he apply his mind to the commands of Christ and aim to keep them? Or, to put the last question another way, does he see himself as under orders? Does he view himself as the *servant* of God? If he utterly fails any one of these tests his Christianity is in serious doubt. If, on the other hand, he finds these things in himself *in some degree*, his assurance ought to grow. He has taken a further step toward 'full assurance'.

The tests I have outlined above are so simple that I imagine you have applied them to yourself even as you have been reading. I certainly hope that you have done so. They are for every professing Christian. No one is excluded.

But suppose you have failed these tests, what then? Your case is serious, but not hopeless. It is serious because you may have thought that Christ saves men without changing them. This entire book is written to show that such a position is false. The Lord Jesus warned:

> Many will say to me on that day, 'Lord, Lord, did we not prophesy in your name, and in your name drive out demons and perform many miracles?' Then I will tell them plainly, 'I never knew you. Away from me, you evildoers!' (*Matthew 7:22–23*)

A man would be a fool to ignore these words from the Saviour. I plead with you not to do so.

But there *is* hope. God's command to each of us is to turn from our sins and to trust in Jesus Christ to save us. Note the two parts to this prescription. First, in intention we must have done with sin once for all. Why do I say 'in intention?' Because God does not require us to *promise* that we will never again sin. Such a promise would be made in pride and arrogance. We have no power to conquer sin except as God gives it to us moment by moment. No, the question is not about how we shall stand toward the practice of sin at some future date. God wants to know what our desire is now. Do we want to have done with sin for ever? Every sin, not just one or two that particularly embarrass us! Is that our earnest longing *right now*? If it is, we have turned from sin. In the language of Scripture, we have repented.

Second, we must turn to Jesus Christ in faith. That means two things. (1) We must accept God's description of Christ as we find it in His Word. We must believe that Jesus Christ is the unique Son of God. (2) We must trust Him to save us, not leaning on our own supposed good works or merits, but solely on Him. To believe in ourselves, in our good resolutions or in our own abilities and works, is idolatry. To believe in Jesus Christ gives God the glory of our salvation. To believe in Jesus Christ is to find peace with God.

4: *God at Work*

If you are a believer here is a truth of first importance: God is at work in you. God has always worked in believers to make them like Christ. He did so in Old Testament days. He does so in New Testament days. Never have God's people been left to themselves to be spiritual or carnal. In all ages God has been active in them to make them habitually godly. And God never fails!

Look at Psalm 1 for example. There the writer contrasts two kinds of men. He speaks of the man who delights 'in the law of the Lord.' He also speaks of the 'wicked.' Two categories – no more. Why? Why not discuss the men who are saved but do not delight in God's law? The answer is clear: 'over the long haul' there are no such men. So far as a man's life-span is concerned he falls into one of two groups. Only conversion can move him from one category to the other. And there is nothing in between. No third group exists.

Of course, that godly man may lapse temporarily into deep sin. Look at King David – an adulterer and worse! Even his death-bed is marred by bitterness. What a damnable thing sin is – even that sin that remains in a child of God! How desperately we need God's mercy day by day! We dare not lose sight of that.

Still, the fact remains: all men are *characteristically* godly or ungodly. Two classes – that is all. At the end of the Psalm we meet them again.

The Lord watches over the way of the righteous, but the way of the wicked will perish. (*1:6*)

Some think that this first psalm is an introduction to the whole book of Psalms. If so, it serves us notice at the outset that the Psalms will treat men as either godly or ungodly. There will be no middle ground. And that is precisely what we find. Psalm 15, for instance, opens with a question, 'Lord, who may dwell in your sanctuary? Who may live on your holy hill?' The next verse answers, 'He whose walk is blameless and who does what is righteous.' That man shall live in God's presence – that man and no other!

The New Testament teaches the same truth. Even before we meet the Lord Jesus we hear an angel describing Christ's work. To Joseph he says:

You are to give him the name Jesus, because he will save his people from their sins. (*Matthew 1:21*)

It is wrong to make this mean nothing more than that Jesus will save His people from the punishment of their sins. He will do that, and much more! He came to call sinners to repentance. That is, He came to call sinners to change their minds about the attractiveness of sin. When a sinner does that – and he can only do that with Christ's saving help – he has repented. But when he finds sin unattractive, when he begins to loath the impulse to break God's laws, he must not think that he has brought himself to this attitude toward sin. No, even his repentance is the work of God. It is a part of his being saved from sin. Nor is it a one-time event. He repents again and again as days and years come and go, always with God's help. Paul put it this way:

Continue to work out your salvation with fear and trembling, for it is God who works in you to will and to act according to his good purpose. (*Philippians 2:12–13*)

When our salvation works itself out in our daily lives, God is the cause. He works in us, first to will, and then to do what we ought to will and to do. To put it another way: throughout our Christian lives Christ is saving us from our sins. He does it by moving us to choose what is pleasing to God.

Paul made this point another way. To the same church he wrote:

> Being confident of this, that he who began a good work in you will carry it on to completion until the day of Christ Jesus. (*Philippians 1:6*)

Have we sometimes felt that the God who saved us will meet us at the end of our lives, but in the meantime we are very frequently left on our own to make progress or to fall back? Not at all, says Paul. God began the good work in us. He keeps up the work till Christ returns. Then He will complete it. What a God! What a Saviour!

Scripture hammers on this theme. Let us hear Paul again:

> For it is by grace you have been saved, through faith – and this not from yourselves, it is the gift of God – not by works, so that no one can boast. (*Ephesians 2:8–9*)

Those are familiar verses. Many of us have memorised them. But notice how Paul completes his thought.

> For we are God's workmanship, created in Christ Jesus to do good works, which God prepared in advance for us to do. (*Ephesians 2:10*)

God made us to do His will. All Christians agree with that. But here is the point. He did not simply *hope* that we would walk in His will. He knew fallen man too well for that. No! He also 'before ordained' (KJV) that we should walk in His will, doing good works. He did not leave it to chance. He made up His mind that we would walk as He wanted us to walk. 'We are God's handiwork,' says the New English Bible, 'created in Christ Jesus to devote ourselves to the good deeds for which God has designed us.'

But someone may ask, 'Didn't God create Adam to serve Him, and didn't Adam fall? Doesn't that show that God's design is no guarantee that we will keep up our good works?' Such a question brings us to the very heart of Christianity. The key to the difference between Adam and the Christian is in the phrase, 'created in Christ Jesus.' Let us give it a closer look.

God designed Adam to stand trial for humanity. Life or death both for himself and the whole race were made dependent upon his obedience or disobedience. We know too well what Adam did. He chose death, not for himself only but for us all. Since Adam, all men in this world are 'dead in . . . transgressions and sins' (*Ephesians 2:1*). Our Lord is the only exception. This is an awful fact, brought about by Adam's sin. We dare not tone it down or treat it with indifference.

Why was Adam able to fail? *Because he was not 'created in Christ Jesus.'* Adam was part of the old creation, as we all were. It was a beautiful creation when it came from the hand of God. In some ways it still is. But morally and spiritually it is now dead. There is no spiritual life at all in the old world, the old creation. The deadly bite of sin is everywhere. But alongside the old creation is another world, *the new creation.* And this is the world a man enters when he is created in Christ Jesus. The believer is a new man inhabiting a new world. Or, as Paul put it, 'If anyone is in Christ, he is a new creation' (*2 Corinthians 5:17*).

Now here comes the important point. Like Adam, Jesus Christ stood trial for all who would ever belong to Him. But, unlike Adam, He stood the test! And it is His will to give to His people the benefits of the victory He has won. As He died for them, so too does He live again for them. That means that a believer does not wait until he dies to receive the fruits of Christ's life and death and resurrection. Not at all! He begins to conquer sin and Satan from the day when he becomes a believer. That is what it means to be 'created in Christ Jesus.' The Christian is made one with Christ at the very outset of his new life, so that he will do what is right. God has not made His *new* creation for another fall! That is how it differs from the old. No, we are 'God's handiwork' in order that we may succeed! What a great God we have! And what a great Saviour!

The apostle James tells us the same thing. Who of us has not wrestled with his words, 'Faith by itself, if it is not accompanied by action, is dead' (*James 2:17*)? James speaks sharply. 'Faith without deeds is useless' (*2:20*)! He means that a godly life always accompanies real faith. Other faith is dead. It cannot bring a man to God. Do you propose to show true faith without good works? Even the dead faith of devils produces one 'work' – they 'shudder' (*2:19*)! Can faith be real that has no works at all? Never! James denies it absolutely.

Of course James, like Paul and John, is talking about the tenor of our lives. He recognises that in single acts we may offend God. He says of himself and us, 'We all stumble in many ways' (*James 3:2*). Only when we go to be with the Lord shall we become completely perfect. Until then our lives will be *characterised by righteousness but marred by sin.*

The Book of Hebrews stresses the same truth. After a severe warning to professed Christians, we read this:

> Even though we speak like this, dear friends, we are confident of better things in your case – things that accompany salvation. (*Hebrews 6:9*)

So then, there are things that always accompany salvation! There are clues to the reality of a man's profession. What are they? They are good works. Why do they accompany salvation? Because God only saves good men? Not at all! They go hand in hand with salvation because the God that saves also works in His people to make them like His Son. And the work can be seen. Listen to the writer of Hebrews again, where he spells out what he means:

> God is not unjust; he will not forget your work and the love you have shown him as you have helped his people and continue to help them. (*Hebrews 6:10*)

Believers are not yet perfect. They are not beyond the need for warnings. They cannot boast in themselves. They can, however, be helped and encouraged in the very same way that the writer of Hebrews indicates. We can say, 'Dear friends, we are confident of better things in your case – things that accompany salvation!' A frequent theme of my preaching must be: Christian, take heart: God is at work in you!

Let me call one more witness – the Apostle Peter. Here he is following up a warning to professed Christians by describing those who fall away:

> Of them the proverbs are true: 'A dog returns to its vomit' and, 'A sow that is washed goes back to her wallowing in the mud.' (*2 Peter 2:22*)

Why does the dog return to his vomit? Because he is a dog! It is his nature to do so. Why does the sow run back to the mud hole and plunge in? Because she is a sow! Her nature calls for mire. You may clean her up. You may put a bow under her chin. If, however, you get her within whiffing distance of a mud hole you have lost her! She will dash away from you and jump in. She will wallow in the mud just because she is a pig and not a man.

The difference between a pig and a man is *not* that a pig

will fall in the mud and a man will not. No, that is not the difference at all. A man may also fall into the mire. The difference is that the man will not feel at home there. He will get out.

So it is with the Christian. A true believer may fall into the mud of sin. Much to his shame, he may do the vilest thing. He may grieve his Saviour fearfully. He may quench the Holy Spirit. He may try the Father's love to the utmost. All of us know from bitter experience that what I am saying is true. But there is a difference between the true believer and the mere professor. It is this. The believer will not be content to stay in that condition. God has given him a new nature. God will be at work in his heart. He may struggle and all but fight against divine intervention, but God will pluck him out of the mud and bring him back into fellowship with Himself. The Christian will not stay in the mire where the mere professor may be satisfied. Christian, take heart!

What, then, is a 'carnal' Christian? Is it biblical to divide believers into 'spiritual men' and 'carnal men'? There is, I think, a better way. It would be better to say that each believer is both spiritual and carnal. Even that, however, is not quite what the New Testament teaches. It is best to emphasise what the Bible emphasises: Christians are habitually, or characteristically, spiritual men and women. If a man is not characteristically spiritual he is not a Christian at all. No amount of profession will make up for his ungodliness. But it is true of genuine believers, *in a sense*, that we are carnal. It is true, I mean, that we still sometimes sin. We are in constant need of God's mercy. We are always candidates for God's grace.

In what sense is a Christian carnal? I have tried to answer that question in chapter two. Right now, however, I want you to get a firm hold on this glorious fact: if you are a Christian, God is at work in you!

5: *Abiding in Christ*

Some men persist in dividing Christians into two groups, 'spiritual' Christians, and 'carnal' Christians. Where did they get that idea? Where did I get it? Where did you get it, if you hold it? Usually the answer is that we thought we got it from the Bible. But where in the Bible? One common answer is John chapter 15, where Jesus shows the importance of abiding in Him.

Let us look at John 15:4–5. Here, if anywhere, we will find Christians divided into two groups. Jesus is speaking:

> Remain in me, and I will remain in you. No branch can bear fruit by itself; it must remain in the vine. Neither can you bear fruit unless you remain in me. I am the vine; you are the branches. If a man remains in me and I in him, he will bear much fruit; apart from me you can do nothing.

A common way to explain these verses goes like this: 'There are two kinds of Christians, those who abide (remain) in Christ and bring forth much fruit, and those who do not abide (do not remain) in Christ and bring forth little or no fruit.' The teacher may then go on to ask, 'What kind of Christian are you? Are you abiding or remaining in Christ? Are you a fruitful Christian? Or is your life wasted because you do not abide in Him?'

Taken alone, these verses might seem to speak of two classes of Christians. Naturally, as a believer in Christ you would want to be in the 'fruitful' class. A man who is a

Christian will want to be the best kind of servant to Jesus. God help us if we are content to be less than He tells us to be!

These verses have a context, however. When we look at the passage as a whole we find that Jesus does not have two grades of Christians in mind. In verse 2 he shows that He is dealing with unbelievers as well. Speaking of the Father, Jesus says, 'He cuts off every branch in me that bears no fruit.' Again, in verse 6 He says, 'If anyone does not remain in me, he is like a branch that is thrown away and withers; such branches are picked up, thrown into the fire and burned.'

There are two classes of men here, but are they both Christians? Will God cast out believers? Will God do something to Christians that is comparable to the burning of branches? A branch is not saved by fire, as gold may be. A branch is destroyed by fire – forever! Will the Father destroy real believers? Never!

There are indeed two kinds of men here. Of both Jesus says, 'They are *in me*.' The phrase 'in me' suggests that He is speaking of real Christians. Would Jesus say of an unbeliever, 'He is in me'? Strange as it may seem, the answer is 'Yes'.

There is a principle here that will help you in your Bible study from now on; the principle that *the Bible often addresses men according to what they profess*. If a man claims to be a believer, the Bible will speak to him as a believer; if he claims to be a saint, the Bible will call him a saint; if he claims to be 'in Christ,' the Bible will speak to him as 'in Christ.' Odd as this may sound, there are examples all through the New Testament.

In Matthew 12:49, for instance, Jesus pointed to His disciples and said, 'Here are . . . my brothers!' All those disciples professed to be His 'brothers'. But were they? Not all of them! Judas Iscariot was no doubt there.

Perhaps the group included some of those 'disciples' that turned away from Him in great numbers later on. Jesus calls this group 'brothers'. But He says more. He adds, 'Whoever does the will of my Father in heaven is my brother . . .' (*12:50*). That is the insignia of true 'brothers'. 'You are my brothers by profession,' He might have said, 'but make sure of it by doing the will of God!'

The New Testament uses the title 'disciple' in the same way. In John 6:64 Jesus speaks to 'disciples' (compare 6:61). He says, 'There are some of you who do not believe.' This offended these 'disciples' and they turned on their heels and left. They were disciples *by profession*, but that was all. That is why John adds,

> From this time many of his disciples turned back and no longer followed him. (*John 6:66*)

Profession and possession are not the same thing.

The Bible sometimes calls men believers, who prove to be unsaved. Listen to this:

> Now while [Jesus] was in Jerusalem at the Passover Feast, many people saw the miraculous signs he was doing and believed in his name. But Jesus would not entrust himself to them, for he knew all men. (*John 2:23–24*)

Oddly enough, the word translated 'entrust' in verse 24 is the same word translated 'believe' in verse 23. You might say, 'They believed in Him, but He didn't believe in them!' They claimed to be believers. They were believers *by profession*. But Jesus knew their hearts. His judgment was that they were not *true* believers at all! And John adds: 'He knew what was in man' (*John 2:25. Cf. also John 8:30–37*).

Paul and others use the same principle. They address men according to their profession. Paul writes to the 'saints' at Rome. Did Paul mean to imply that all in the

Roman church were saved? Did he propose to speak only to the true believers in that church? In both cases the answer is 'No'.

Paul gave these 'saints' the title they claimed for themselves. If a man claims to be a Christian he is claiming to be a saint. He is claiming to be a believer. No doubt that church was largely made up of true saints. But listen to this:

> Because of your stubbornness and your unrepentant heart, you are storing up wrath against yourself for the day of God's wrath, when his righteous judgment will be revealed! (*Romans 2:5*)

Was that spoken of true saints? Evidently not! Nor was it of true believers that Paul said, 'If you live according to the sinful nature, you will die' (*Romans 8:13*). He wrote that to everyone in Rome who *professed* faith. But when he had only true believers in view he said, 'You . . . are controlled, not by the sinful nature but by the Spirit' (*Romans 8:9*).

The writer of Hebrews does the same thing. To men he calls 'holy brothers' (*Hebrews 3:1*) he gives this awful warning:

> See to it, brothers, that none of you has a sinful, unbelieving heart that turns away from the living God. (*Hebrews 3:12*)

'Holy brothers' would not have 'sinful, unbelieving' hearts. But *professed* 'holy brothers' certainly might have such hearts. Yet he calls them 'holy brothers' without hesitation.

In the same way James speaks to men he calls 'my brothers' (*James 2:14*). But note what else he says:

> You believe that there is one God. Good! Even the demons believer that – and shudder. *You foolish man,* do

[45]

you want evidence that faith without deeds is useless? (*James 2:19–20*)

All of the men to whom James wrote were his 'brothers' by profession. They claimed to be 'brothers', so he called them brothers. But after giving them the title they claimed, James goes on to speak to them as a mixed group. He scatters warnings, as well as encouragements, with both hands.

With this principle in mind let us look back at John 15. Jesus spoke to professed followers. 'All right,' he said in effect, 'let's assume that you are *in me*. Let's say you are vitally connected to me. Now here is the acid test. Will you stay with me, and prove to be true? Or will you wither and be cast away?' Those were the two possibilities. There was no third way. Some would persevere, abide, and be fruitful. Some would be cut off. There was no middle group. There *is* no middle group today.

Would some, then, lose their salvation? Would some who were genuinely converted fail to abide or remain in Christ? Not at all! Listen to John again.

No one who lives (abides) in him keeps on sinning. No one who continues to sin has either seen him or known him. (*1 John 3:6*)

How many groups do you see in this verse? There are just two. John speaks of those who live in Christ, who abide in Him. These are men and women and children who do *not* keep on sinning. They make up the first group. But then he tells us of another set of people. They are the men and women and children who continue to sin. Not one of these, John says, 'has either seen him or known him.' In other words, there are none who once knew Him and now do not. There are none lost who once were saved. Two groups, and no more! To put it as plainly as I know how:

every one who has been saved abides in Christ! God's people are kept 'abiding' by the power of God. Christian, take heart!

Let me pause for a moment. I want to imagine your reaction to what I have written. The reaction I fear most is the one that says, 'This is too good to be true!' That takes the discussion out of the arena of what the Bible teaches. In its place it puts the question, 'How do I *feel* about what the author says?' Note this carefully. John, writing by inspiration of the Spirit of God, recognises only two types of men in the world. There are those who abide in Christ, and those who have never seen Him or known Him. That is all; there are no others.

Another reaction, I think, will go like this: 'Well, maybe he's right about John 15, but what about all these *worldly* Christians? We need to talk about them!' In one way or another, we insist on having two groups of believers. If we cannot call them 'carnal and spiritual,' or 'abiders and non-abiders,' perhaps we can call them 'worldly and non-worldly.'

What does the Bible say about 'worldly Christians?' Nothing at all! The worldliness the Bible describes is incompatible with Christianity. You can be worldly, or you can be a Christian. You cannot be both. Listen to John again.

> Do not love the world or anything in the world. If anyone loves the world, *the love of the Father is not in him.* (*1 John 2:15*)

There are two kinds of men here, and only two. There are men who love the Father; there are men who love the world. The men who love the world do not have the love of the Father in them. In other words, they are unsaved. Saved men do not love the world!

Keep in mind that this verse, like the others we have

looked at, speaks of the tenor of our lives. A Christian may do something that is 'worldly.' In fact, all Christians fail to live perfectly non-worldly lives. But this is the point: there is no basis here for dividing Christians into two groups. The Christian who points at another believer and says, 'He is worldly,' is himself sometimes 'worldly' in the same sense. If any man is worldly in the other sense, *if any man loves the world*, he is not a Christian at all. On the other hand, I am not denying that there are differing degrees in which Christians succeed in overcoming the world. Not at all! No two believers have come to the same level of maturity. No two Christians progress at the same rate. All of that is true, and we must not forget it. But the difference is one of *degree*, not of *kind*. It always remains true that the tenor of a Christian's life is godliness. And that is true of every believer without exception. There are no characteristically worldly Christians. Not even one!

I wish I could make you feel the wonder of what I am saying. I cannot say it too often. God is at work in each of His people! Literally millions of hours have been spent trying to get Christians to 'let' God work. Most of it has been wasted. I do not say all of it. God uses exhortation. He uses preaching and instruction. 'All Scripture,' Paul wrote, 'is . . . useful for . . . rebuking, correcting . . .' (*2 Timothy 3:16*). So believers must be rebuked and corrected in a scriptural way. And true Christians will respond. Because God is at work in them, it will not be long before they are back on the track.

Much of the time we have spent exhorting Christians has been wasted. It would have been better for us to warn men that if God is not at work in them they are not saved. They may attend Bible-believing churches. They may be *active* members. They may be well thought of by godly men. But are they saved? That is the question. And note this carefully: we cannot find the answer simply by

[48]

pointing to a date when they accepted Christ. Their lives, like mine and yours, must pass the test of going on with Christ. Perseverance is necessary. Our profession is a sham without it. But if we are Christians, we are not left to ourselves. God is at work in us. He will make sure that we make progress. He is determined that not one of His people shall ever fail the test!

Sad to say, there are still other ways in which certain people divide Christians into groups. Let me mention one more: 'Spirit-filled and non-Spirit-filled' believers. This division is so important that I want to spend my next chapter on it.

But first let me add a word about self-satisfaction. Certain good men who read and teach the Bible are fearful of what I have said. They are afraid to say to Christians, 'God is at work in each of you!.' They are rightly concerned about the effect of such a statement. I do not blame them. I do not blame you for asking how this truth will affect you, if you accept it. Surely every parent must ask, 'What will be the effect on my child if I teach him this?'

Let me lay down a helpful principle: all truths have their dangers. There are no harmless truths. Any truth, *taught to the exclusion of other truths*, will lead us to pervert God's Word. Here is an example: Jesus is a man. That is true, is it not? It is a truth vital to our salvation. Sinners needed a *man* to die for them. An angel could not do so.

But note what unconverted theologians have done with that truth. They have taught that Jesus was a man and have left out the fact that He is God. By teaching one truth to the exclusion of the other they have perverted God's Word. And they have blasphemed our Saviour.

Consider the truth of the believer's security in Christ. We rejoice in it. But can you imagine a more dangerous truth? It must be balanced by the fact that God is at work in each of His people. Otherwise, it is an encouragement to sin. If I give a Christian a licence to sin I have twisted God's Word beyond recognition. Listen to Paul.

> What shall we say, then? Shall we go on sinning so that grace may increase? By no means! We died to sin; how can we live in it any longer? (*Romans 6:1–2*)

Here is the point: we are not to preach *safe* truth; we are to preach *all* truth.

The doctrine that God is at work in each of His people includes this fact: God is at work to keep us from self-satisfaction. We do not reach a level of Christianity with which we may be satisfied. If a man stays content with the level he has reached, that man is not a Christian. I used the word *stays* deliberately. I do not mean that we are never smug and self-satisfied. Sadly, we sometimes are. But – thank God! – He will not leave us there.

God has His own ways of weaning us from self-satisfaction. One of them is connected with our remaining sinfulness. A Christian longs for holiness. He hungers and thirsts after righteousness. God has made him that way. We are not yet perfect, however. We are forcibly reminded of that when we sin. Our sin grieves us, if we are Christians. We fight it. We wrestle with self. We cry with Paul, 'What a wretched man I am!' (*Romans 7:24*). And we shall keep on crying out until Christ returns.

> We ourselves, who have the firstfruits of the Spirit, groan inwardly as we wait eagerly for our adoption as sons, the redemption of our bodies. (*Romans 8:23*)

Sin no longer characterised Paul's life, but he longed to be done with it completely. He thirsted after perfection. And so does every true believer.

I want to mention one more way that God keeps us from being puffed up over his work in us. We read about it in 2 Corinthians 12, where Paul describes an unusual experience. He had been taken up into heaven. There he heard words too marvellous to be repeated to men. What a fine affair to cause a man to swell with pride!

Did Paul become puffed up? No! Listen as he tells us why.

> To keep me from becoming conceited because of these surpassingly great revelations, there was given me a thorn in my flesh, a messenger of Satan, to torment me. (*2 Corinthians 12:7*)

What happened? God gave Paul a thorn in the flesh!

I know what you are thinking: that was not God, it was Satan! But wait. Look again at the words, 'To keep me from becoming conceited.' Was Satan worried that Paul would become conceited and useless to God? Hardly! It was God who protected Paul from self-satisfaction. God did it – but He used Satan! God knew Satan's motives. And God knew that Satan wanted to hurt Paul. In addition, God knew what Satan did not know. God knew that a 'thorn', whatever it was, was just what Paul needed at this point. So God let Satan give it to Paul, *but it was a gift from God*!

Our circumstances are not accidents. Some come directly from God. Some come through godly men. Some are worked out for us by the ungodly. Some are the work of Satan and his forces. Nevertheless, God is in control of them all. Each event in a Christian's life is given by God. Why? For a thousand reasons, I suppose. One important aim is to wean us from self-satisfaction. And be sure of this: God knows exactly how to do it!

6: *The Spirit-Filled Life*

The most popular way to divide Christians is to speak of
'Spirit-filled' Christians and of Christians who are not
'Spirit-filled.' Men that differ widely in other ways agree
on this: what we need are more Spirit-filled believers.
Publications ranging from tracts and pamphlets to books
of hundreds of pages have been written to show Christians
how to be filled with the Spirit. It seems to be assumed
almost everywhere that the average Christian is *not*
Spirit-filled. I am devoting an entire chapter to this
assumption because I want to take it seriously.

First, we will need a definition. What does it mean to be
'Spirit-filled'? We know who the Holy Spirit is, but what
does the word 'filled' mean? That is the heart of the
question.

To 'fill' something, of course, means to take up, or
occupy, all the space in it. That is the literal sense of the
word 'fill'. In John 19:29 (KJV) we read, 'They filled a
sponge with vinegar.' This is a good example of the literal
use. But we are interested in another way of using the
word 'fill'. There are quite a few instances in the Bible
where *a person* is said to be 'filled' with something. The
idea in those cases is *not* that all the empty space in his
body has been filled with some other substance. That is
not the point at all.

A person is said to be 'filled' with something when that
thing, whatever it is, possesses him so as to control what
he does. For example, when the disciples understood that

Jesus was about to be crucified, He said to them: 'Because I have said these things, you are filled with grief' (*John 16:6*). Grief had taken control of these men and their sadness was evident to Jesus. They could not hide it. Their grief had the upper hand, and it showed.

Here is another illustration:

> Now a man named Ananias, together with his wife Sapphira, also sold a piece of property. With his wife's full knowledge he kept back part of the money for himself, but brought the rest and put it at the apostles' feet. Then Peter said, 'Ananias, how is it that Satan has so *filled* your heart that you have lied to the Holy Spirit and have kept for yourself some of the money you received for the land? Didn't it belong to you before it was sold? And after it was sold, wasn't the money at your disposal? What made you think of doing such a thing? You have not lied to men but to God.' When Ananias heard this, he fell down and died. (*Acts 5:1–5*)

Why did Ananias lie? Peter said, 'Satan has . . . filled your heart.' When Ananias planned his lie he was under the control of Satan. 'To fill his heart' was to control him.

Let me give you one more example. Paul is speaking here:

> Since [the world] did not think it worthwhile to retain the knowledge of God, he gave them over to a depraved mind, to do what ought not to be done. They have become *filled* with every kind of wickedness, evil, greed and depravity. They are *full of* envy, murder, strife, deceit and malice. (*Romans 1:28–29*)

Paul's point is clear. Since God has given men over to a depraved mind, they are under its control. And what happens? They show their depravity. It works out in their actions. To be filled with evil is to be controlled by it. We use the same figure of speech in English. We say, for instance, that a man is 'filled with rage.' We mean that, at that moment or in that hour, rage is controlling his actions. Once more, to be filled is to be controlled.

Now the same thing is true when a man is said to be *'filled with the Holy Spirit.'* The idea is that what he is about to do, or the attitudes that he is about to display, are the work of the Spirit of God. To be filled with the Spirit is to be controlled by the Spirit.

And that brings us to the question, 'Are all believers Spirit-filled?'

Let me tell you why we must be especially careful in answering this question. In this case a simple 'yes' or 'no' will not do. Here's why. The Bible uses the idea of Spirit-filling in at least two different ways. If we do not keep them distinct we shall be confused. I know this from sad personal experience. For some years, in writing and speaking on this subject, I failed to make these distinctions. The result was that I failed to tell the whole truth. I do not want to repeat that mistake.

Let me start with two words: *service* and *sanctification*. If I apply these to the filling with the Spirit I think you will begin to grasp what I am talking about. Throughout the Bible the Spirit 'fills' men to perform some service. Here is an example:

Then Moses said to the Israelites, 'See, the Lord has chosen Bezalel . . . and he has *filled* him with the Spirit of God, with skill, ability and knowledge in all kinds of crafts – to make artistic designs . . . And he has given both him and Oholiab . . . the ability to teach others. He has *filled* them with skill to do all kinds of work as craftsmen, designers, embroiderers in blue, purple and scarlet yarn and fine linen, and weavers – all of them master craftsmen and designers. So Bezalel, Oholiab and every skilled person to whom the Lord has given skill and ability to know how to carry out all the work of constructing the sanctuary are to do the work just as the Lord has commanded.' (*Exodus 35:30–36:1*)

Note that this passage is about *service* for God. It is about the building of the tabernacle. It has nothing to do with the moral quality, the *sanctification*, of Bezalel and the others. What is important here is what they could do, not what they were. Perhaps they were fine men. We do not know. But they were filled with the Spirit in order to do the work. That is all we are told.

In this sense, an unconverted man might be filled with the Spirit! The New Testament shows that Balaam was a wicked man (*2 Peter 2:15; Jude 11; Revelation 2:14*). But 'the Spirit of God came upon him' (*Numbers 24:2*), and he prophesied. And the prophecy he uttered was true. Balaam had a work to do for God and he did it. His power, however, was not his own. It came from the Spirit of God. He was a tool in the Spirit's hand. King Saul in the Old Testament (*1 Samuel 16:14*), and Judas Iscariot in the New, seem to be instances of the same thing.

When we come to the New Testament the issue of being filled with the Spirit for service becomes quite prominent. The work, or service, of carrying the gospel through all the world is a dominant theme. References to Spirit-filling are often connected with the spread of the good news. We see this in the Book of Acts. Acts 4 tells us that Peter and John, after being released from custody for preaching Christ, reported that they had been commanded to be silent. This led the disciples to pray. Here is a portion of their prayer and its result:

Now, Lord, consider their threats and enable your servants to speak your word with great boldness . . . After they prayed, the place where they were meeting was shaken. And they were all *filled* with the Holy Spirit and spoke the word of God boldly. (*Acts 4:29,31*)

They prayed to be given boldness. The Lord answered by filling them with His Spirit. And the result was: they 'spoke the word of God boldly.' A later verse adds, 'More and more men and women believed in the Lord' (*Acts 5:14*).

We learn here that success, in the sense of fruit for our labours, follows the filling of the Spirit. We must be controlled by the Spirit of God to be able to do God's work effectively. We would do well to pray for this 'filling of the Spirit' constantly. God's work depends upon it. None of us may simply assume that we are 'Spirit-filled', in this sense. We need a deeper measure of the control of the Spirit than we have ever before experienced. We need *revival*. Revival is the result of the church being filled with God's Holy Spirit for service. Let us cry out to God for it!

This then is the filling of the Spirit *for service*. Let me add a few words of caution to help you think about it. First, this is not something that God is always pleased to give. We must cry to God for it! But it is in God's hand to give this filling or to withhold it. It has pleased Him to put some of His choicest servants in dry places, to labour without fruit for many years. Paul, for example, was wonderfully successful in some cities, but not in all. At Lystra he did one notable work. But what then? The crowd turned on him. The Holy Spirit, who might have melted the hearts of all God's enemies, did not do so. The 'power' was not given. Paul's opponents got the upper hand. They stoned him. Then they dragged him outside the city and left him for dead. No doubt he longed to be used by the Spirit in Lystra in a triumphant way. But that was not to be. God gives this 'filling' sovereignly. That is the first thing to remember.

My second caution is this: we must not suppose that we have found two kinds of Christians here. This is not a moral issue. We do not measure the believer's spirituality by the measure of his success. If God sends revival through one of us, we must not think that we have outstripped our brothers in godliness. No! God will send by whom He pleases. Let us hunger and thirst to be filled with His Spirit for service. But God sends His Spirit to refresh us in His own time, according to His own will. There are no magic formulas for revival. We cannot command it. We may await it with longing, and we are bound to express our longing in prayer.

But now I want to move on to the filling of the Spirit for *sanctification*. Here again we are looking at the control of the Spirit, but for a different purpose. The issue now is not the success of our service, but the success of our growth in godliness. These two things, of course, are not unrelated. But it is this second thing, the success of our growth in godliness, that this book is about.

Not long ago I heard a speaker quote the Puritan theologian, John Owen. Owen had somewhere written something like this: 'The Holy Spirit is always the Spirit of Holiness, but He is not always the Spirit of Comfort'. The point seemed to be that the Spirit always works to make us holy, but He does not always labour to give us the comfort we would like to have. And I have no doubt that Owen was right. Though I have received much comfort in my Christian life, the discipline of the Lord has been anything but 'comfortable' at times. During those seasons the Spirit was at work to make me like the Lord Jesus, but He was content to postpone some of my comfort to a later day.

Here is the point: all Christians are characteristically Spirit-filled, or Spirit-controlled, when we are talking about growth in godliness. This truth is already implied by the fact that there are no carnal, or worldly, believers. The Holy Spirit Himself sees to that!

The Spirit, we must understand, is not always the Spirit

of the special graces connected with revival. He is not at every moment the Spirit of Comfort in each believer. Some of His influences come and go. But He is always the Spirit of Holiness. That may be, in part, why He is called the *Holy* Spirit.

But is every believer characteristically Spirit-filled? Here is a portion of John's Gospel to help us answer the question:

> Jesus stood and said in a loud voice, 'If any man is thirsty, let him come to me and drink. Whoever believes in me, as the Scripture has said, streams of living water will flow from within him.' By this he meant the Spirit, whom those who believed in him were later to receive. Up to that time the Spirit had not been given, since Jesus had not yet been glorified. (*John 7:37–39*)

Earlier, I told you how I once robbed Christians of this promise. Jesus' statement is not about one select group. Not at all! It is a statement of fact about all believers. If we look at it closely we can see what it was that I wanted to take away from God's people. Exactly what does this passage promise?

John himself tells us what the streams of living water mean. They represent the Holy Spirit. Listen: 'By this he meant the Spirit.' There can be no argument here. But Jesus implies much more. The picture is not of a trickling brook; much less is it a picture of a stagnant pool. No, Jesus speaks of streams or rivers of living water. (This is the common Greek word for 'river'.) He deliberately chose His figure to suggest fulness, abundance, a cup running over! That is why those who teach a special 'filling with the Spirit' almost always appeal to this verse. They understand that Jesus is describing an abundance.

Most Christians agree that every believer has the Holy Spirit in some sense. Often this is called 'the dwelling of the Holy Spirit in the believer.' Why not apply this verse to His 'dwelling' in the believer? For good reason: something more than 'dwelling' is suggested here. This is a picture of overflowing fulness. No other condition will explain the 'streams (rivers) of living water!'

Is it true, then, that the Spirit 'dwells in' some believers, but 'fills' others? Not at all! The truth is this: He dwells in all believers. To what extent? He 'fills' them. 'Filling' describes how He dwells in the Christian. The Holy Spirit does not live in one small corner of the Christian's life; He fills it. Nor is that all. He fills it to overflowing! Christian, take heart!

Let me pause here to avoid misunderstanding. I have not said, and I do not believe, that the Spirit fills the Christian for every purpose. Remember that to 'fill' means to 'control'. God does *not* control you and me for every purpose. He may take control of you to bring many to Himself, as He filled Peter and Paul in Acts. And He may not do that with me at all. But one thing is perfectly clear from John 7:37–39. In some sense, for some purpose, the Spirit fills (controls) every child of God. And He does not do so meagrely. He fills to overflowing! Of course this 'fulness' is not absolute, as though there were no further room for God to work. John is speaking comparatively. New Testament believers overflow with the Spirit compared with believers before Pentecost.

What shall we say, then, about the command: 'Be filled with the Spirit' (*Ephesians 5:18*). Doesn't this imply that Christians are not filled? It looks like it. The verse, however, could as well be translated, 'Keep on being filled with the Spirit.' And I believe that is the right way. It brings out the force of the verb tense Paul used. But that translation implies that believers are filled with the Spirit.

It says this: you are filled, stay filled. Or, more exactly, keep being filled. We are not dealing with a trickle, but a river!

Does this mean that being filled with the Spirit is automatic? If so, why command us to 'keep on being filled?' Automatic? No. It means this: being filled with the Spirit is automatic at the time of our new birth. We are born filled with the Spirit for our sanctification. Our concern is not becoming filled: it is staying filled. Hence the command: 'Keep on being filled with the Spirit!'

Now someone may ask, 'Aren't we back where we started, with two kinds of Christians, those who stay filled and those who don't? Don't we wind up with a special class of "Spirit-filled" Christians, after all? Haven't you just gone the long way around to get to the same point?'

No, I have not! Remember what we found out about 'carnal' Christians. We found this: a Christian may do some things that are rightly called 'carnal'. But there are no characteristically 'carna!' Christians. Believers are characteristically godly men and women, or they are not Christians. A Christian may do things that could be called 'worldly', but there are no characteristically 'worldly' believers. A man or woman who loves the world, John told us, does not have the love of the Father in him or her. Christians are habitually 'unworldly', or they are not Christians.

The same principle holds here. To be Spirit-filled means to be controlled by the Holy Spirit. While we are yet in this life we may do things that grieve the Spirit. We may assert our own authority. At such times we are not Spirit-filled; we are self-propelled. But God will not leave us in that state. We are to be spiritual Christians. God is determined about that! And He has His means! By whatever measures are necessary, He forces our hands from the throttles of our lives. He re-asserts control. Once more we are Spirit-filled. We are characteristically Spirit-filled, or we are not Christians at all.

To be brief, I have used a mechanical illustration. I said, 'He forces our hands from the throttles of our lives.' That shows God at work. But, of course, there is nothing mechanical about how He works. God has an infinite number of ways to do His will. He is not at a loss when He moves to bring us back to Himself. He can woo or whip. He can draw or drive. He can work rapidly or slowly, as He pleases. In other words, He is free to be God! And in His own way, at His own pace, He brings us back.

Pick an average Christian from a Bible-believing church, and what will you get? If you get a real Christian, you will get a Spirit-filled Christian. Why? Because God only saves good men? Not at all! You will get a Spirit-filled believer because God is at work in each of His people. That is why Paul has written, 'Those who are led by the Spirit of God are sons of God' (*Romans 8:14*). No man is led (controlled) so as to be able to say, 'I cannot be wrong!' Every Christian, however, is characteristically led by God's Spirit. On the average, his acts, his thoughts and his motives will be godly. Why? Because he is filled, controlled and led by the Spirit of God!

Now someone may say, 'Wait a minute! If what you say is true, why don't we have more *fruitful* Christians? Why are so many believers *unfruitful*?'

That is an important question. I want to take it seriously. But the first thing to note is this. Almost instinctively we are back to the old division between two sets of Christians, the 'fruitful' and the 'unfruitful'. So I must ask again: does the Bible teach us that we may look for two kinds of believers?

Scripture insists that all Christians are fruitful. Remember Jesus' words, 'If a man remains in me and I in him, he will bear much fruit' (*John 15:5*). Earlier we saw that those who abide or remain in Christ are Christians. 'Remainers' or 'abiders' and 'Christians' are synonymous. There is no group of 'non-abiding' Christians. Again: all Christians are fruitful. But what is fruit? Some have said that Christ means 'soul-winning', the ability to bring others to God. That is the fruit in view. And then they have pointed out that many Christians never win anyone to Christ. Isn't there a problem here?

It seems clear to me that 'soul-winning' is not especially in Christ's mind here. I will tell you why in a moment. But first I want to remind you of something that you already know. It is this: the winning of a man or woman to Christ is not a simple thing. The person who sees another person turn to the Lord Jesus – if indeed anyone sees it happen – is normally the last link in a long chain of influences. Those influences may very well include the words and deeds of many Christians who would never be given the name 'soul-winner' by others around them. Yet they sowed what some other Christian worker reaped. We must never forget that. This came home to me forcefully in reading about the missionary to India, William Carey. He was certainly a soul-winner, was he not? But listen to his own view of his work. He wrote the following on May 24, 1810:

It is now nearly seventeen years since I left England for this country. Since that time I have been witness to an astonishing train of circumstances, which have produced a new appearance of all things relating to the cause of God in these parts. The whole work, however, has been carried on by God in so mysterious a manner, that it would be difficult for any one person to fix on any particular circumstance, and say, 'I am the instrument by which this work has been accomplished' . . . We see the effect; each one rejoices in it; and yet no one can say how it has been wrought.

There is more than humility in that statement. There is a recognition of the complexity of the ways of God.

The Bible has a good deal to say about fruit-bearing. There is no reason to think that soul-winning alone is in the Lord's mind in John 15. There is good reason to think otherwise. Jesus tells us that His Father 'cuts off' the branches that are unfruitful while He 'trims clean' the rest (*John 15:2*). Then He says to the eleven, 'You are already clean' (*John 15:3*). A branch that is cut off is lost. But I know of no one who holds that Christians who are not 'soul-winners' are lost. It seems more likely that Jesus is thinking of the kind of contrast we find in John 13. There, before Judas departed, Jesus said, 'You are clean, though not every one of you' (*John 13:10*). And John adds the telling remark: 'For he knew who was going to betray him, and that was why he said not every one was clean' (*John 13:11*). Judas was the branch to be cut off. The others were trimmed clean. The Father saw to that. And the result was that they were fruitful. If they had been unfruitful they too would have been cut off, because there is no class of unfruitful Christians.

What, then, is fruit? In the New Testament we find that fruit is all the things that we may reasonably expect to follow upon our knowing Christ. The good works and godly attitudes that spring from our salvation are our fruit. And the Spirit who fills us is their author. Paul gives us a partial list in Galatians 5:22–23:

> The fruit of the Spirit is love, joy, peace, patience, kindness, goodness, faithfulness, gentleness and self-control.

No doubt God's people have these things in differing degrees. We do not all progress at the same speed. But the Spirit is alive in every believer, and brings forth fruit. The alternative to the Spirit's activity is death:

You, however, are controlled not by the sinful nature but by the Spirit, if the Spirit of God lives in you. And if anyone does not have the Spirit of Christ, he does not belong to Christ. (*Romans 8:9*)

Those who do not belong to Christ perish. The rest are controlled or filled by the Spirit of God for sanctification, for godliness. And 'the rest' is not some special group of believers. All God's people are filled by the Spirit of God.

7: *The Psychology of Defeat*

The claim that there are two kinds of Christians has led to a *tragedy* and a *heresy*. The tragedy is that Christians have been misled and discouraged. The heresy is that the sufficiency of Christ has been denied. This chapter is about the tragedy. The next chapter will be about the heresy.

There is a widespread feeling today that something is woefully wrong with Christians. It is not simply the fact that believers are not perfect. It is something more than that. The impression is that God's people are worldly. They are thought to be kicking against the Spirit of God. Everywhere we hear the question, 'What can be done to get Christians straightened out?' At the very least I must respond with another question, 'What is the truth about Christians?'

The truth, it seems to me, is this. If by Christians we mean all those who *profess* faith in Christ, then there is much to bewail. But that is not the group of people that I am writing about in this book. My focus is upon those who genuinely belong to Christ, whoever they may be and wherever they are. Is there something wrong with these men and women? I believe that too often there is.

What is wrong with Christians? The answer is, in part: they are discouraged. Not this one or that one, but Christians at large. We have told them every way we know how, 'There are two levels of Christians, and you are on the lower level.' Is it any wonder that they have believed us? It would be a miracle if they had not.

Do you think I exaggerate? I do not. My own experience has led me to this conclusion. Some time ago I attended a well-known Bible Conference. Of approximately thirty messages we heard there, well over half struck this note. And they did not do it softly! Shortly after returning from that conference I received a notice from a pastor in another city, a good man with a fine church. He was starting a class to help Christians 'find themselves'. I quote: 'Sad to say, the average Christian today is not really functioning; he is not performing the function in the body of Christ that God expects him to.' Can that be true? If the average organ in my body were not functioning I could not write about it. I would be dead! Is the body of Christ, then, a corpse? Has it a vital head and paralysed members? Don't tell Paul that!

Comparing the body of Christ to a building, Paul says, 'The whole building is joined together and rises to become a holy temple in the Lord' (*Ephesians 2:21*). These are not the words of a perfectionist who could see no evil in the church. Far from it! Paul knew well enough how to rebuke his fellow believers. But he did not suppose for a moment that *God's work* was about to come crashing down. No, the Lord intended to create a 'holy temple', and that is what He is doing!

Again, Paul likens the body of Christ to a human body. He tells us the importance of being joined to Christ

the Head, from whom the whole body, supported and held together by its ligaments and sinews, grows as God causes it to grow. (*Colossians 2:19*)

In plain English, Paul says, 'Christ's body is doing well, thank you. Its growth is from God!' Without a doubt, if a man is not connected to the Head, he is in trouble. But, then, he is not a Christian.

Of course I do not mean – and I must constantly repeat

this – that Christians are all that they ought to be. Nor do I think for a moment that any believer has room to be self-satisfied. That is the farthest thing from my mind. Please take me quite seriously here! But I do think that the surest way to dishearten God's people is to assert that there are two levels of Christianity and that they are on the lower level. In fact, I can go even further. You do not need to tell them what level they occupy. They will draw that conclusion for themselves!

Let me go a step further. Suppose you tell them that there are two kinds of Christians and that *they* are on the higher level – what then? Well, no doubt, if they believe you, it will give them an emotional and psychological boost. But can they sustain it? I do not think so; not in most cases. Along with all else that God gives his people, He gives them some insight into their own condition. I know that some Christians are ready to defend their own supposed perfection, but most are not. The few that do so, do it by substantially lowering the standard of perfection. They know themselves too well to do otherwise!

How could Christians be discouraged? If they are growing in Christ why should they be downcast? We may look at a growing child for the answer. It is much more common to misinform a child than it is seriously to stunt his growth. Like all of us, the child is an encyclopedia of misinformation. He 'knows' many things that are not so. Yet he grows. He has life. That life expresses itself. At first he cannot sit up; then he does so. Later he walks, he talks, he plays. The average child does all these things and many more. Why? Because he has physical life from God.

That is the way it is with Christians. They have life from God. Not only physical life – spiritual life too. So they grow. They develop. They live out the life they have. Growth, however, is not the only factor in their moods. It is one of many influences. What they are taught is a large ingredient in how they feel.

Let me illustrate this. Tell a healthy man that he is nearly dead. Then have someone else – a doctor, an expert on sickness – tell him the same thing. Have the diagnosis confirmed by a specialist. Would you be surprised if the man began to feel ill? Would you be amazed if he began to think that his prospects were not good? What else could he think? How else could he feel?

Unless my eyes and ears deceive me, this kind of 'treatment' is given to Christians day in and day out. We have 'victorious life' conferences, and 'deeper life' meetings, and 'spiritual life' crusades, and 'revival' services. So often they seem to start with the same premise: there are two levels of Christian life, and the average Christian is on the lower level! A man would need the strength of Samson to withstand this kind of 'treatment'!

Nor is that all. The diet of the local church is frequently flavoured the same way. The entire weight of a lost world may be thrown on the Christian's shoulder each Sunday. He is dished up a generous helping of what God could do, *if* he were only what he ought to be. Souls would be won in great numbers. Programmes would work, missionaries would be sent forth. A lost world would be conquered, *if* he were only what he ought to be. At last, and perhaps not without tears, he breaks down under this 'treatment'. He is brainwashed.

What does he say then? He says just what you have said: *'I guess I wasn't cut out to be one of the spiritual ones. God bless them! I'd like to be one of them, but I can't.'* If you have not said something like that to yourself, you are the exception among believers.

Of course, if he is a real Christian, he cannot rest content there. He is thoroughly disheartened and he feels sinful. It is not right to be downcast. Didn't Paul say,

'Rejoice in the Lord always' (*Philippians 4:4*)? Now what? Now where shall he turn? Perhaps the next stop is the Christian bookstore. A book may be the answer! He is bleeding, but back on his feet. Little does he know what awaits him!

The bookseller is sympathetic. Obviously our Christian friend is living an 'abnormal' Christian life. He needs to enter upon a 'normal' Christian life. By his own admission our pilgrim is 'unspiritual'. And at hand are a half-dozen books on becoming 'Spirit-filled.' The Christian takes one at random. Or he asks a friend which is best. He takes it home with hope. Finding the right guide is half the battle. When he reads the opening line – 'The average Christian is carnal' – he knows it was written for him.

What happens next? Little or nothing. Our friend is told to 'yield to God.' Do this once, it is implied, and all will be well. A new quality of life will begin. But he thought he had yielded, more than once. Nevertheless he will try again. Or he is told to 'appropriate what God has for you.' That makes sense. If God has something for you, take it. But how? 'Just take it!' What does that mean? 'Believe that you have it, and it is yours.' So our Christian friend sets out to 'believe that he has' what he clearly does not have. Can he do it? He may! – the brain is an amazing (but fallen) machine. If he does, he will have temporary 'victory'. If he does not, he will lapse into misery. Or early Monday morning he will be back at the booksellers. After all, he has read only one book. There are five to go!

There is humour in this story only because I am looking back at it. To those going through it, it is not funny at all. Nor is it funny to the bookseller. He tries to know what is on his shelves. He has read these books for that reason, or perhaps because he sees himself as an 'average' Christian. He sees the glint of hope in them. They may not have solved his defeat, but he thinks that was probably his own fault. Maybe our Christian friend will get more out of them.

Here is the problem with all this advice. If a man could do what the books tell him to do, he would already have the 'victory'. Let us suppose that he is unyielded. (I have shown, I trust, that there are no characteristically unyielded Christians.) If he is characteristically unyielded then he is like an unconverted man. It is as if he were unregenerate. And that means that he is without the will or the power to make any spiritual change in his life. If he is unyielded, then that is the very thing over which he needs the 'victory'. To tell him that he may have the 'victory' if he will just yield is to mock him.

Suppose a man has fallen into a pit that adjoins a tall building. 'How can I get out?' he cries. 'Jump over the building,' I tell him. 'In the process you will get out of the pit!' That is a fine answer. It is perfectly true. But if he answered me according to my folly he would say, 'Fool, if I could do that, I wouldn't need your advice!'

Let me illustrate again. Here is a nervous man, twisting and turning on his bed. He cannot get to sleep. What shall I tell him? Suppose I say, 'Lie still, friend. You'll never get to sleep if you keep up that twisting.' Will that help? Job's friends might have thought so, but most men would not. My words are true. If he would 'lie still' he would go to sleep. But that is the problem: he cannot lie still. He might force his body to do so, but his nerves would scream for relief. So he says, 'If I could do that, I would have been asleep long ago.'

At this very point all cures for 'unspirituality' fail. They all require a 'spiritual man' to make them work. In other words, they all need *God already at work*. Any cure that says, 'God will do the rest if you only start the work' is doomed at the outset. Either God is already at work to lead us to do what He commands, or we have yet to be converted.

[70]

But Christian, take heart! God is at work in His people. That is why there are no habitually disobedient believers. That is why there are no characteristically carnal Christians. That is why Christians are usually Spirit-filled or controlled by the Spirit for their own sanctification. Without God at work, we would be without hope.

Here is the key idea: *God does not ask His people to initiate the work in their own lives. Rather, He calls on them to fall in with whatever He is already doing.* The whole New Testament tells us this. Somehow we have lost this key. On all hands we hear, 'You take the first step, and God will do the rest.' Not so! Any parent with an infant will tell you that the first step is the hardest. In the Christian life God undertakes the hardest part.

Why then does God give us commands? Because His commands reflect the things that God is already at work to accomplish in our lives. We may miss that! God does not say it each time He gives a command. But it is true.

Philippians 2:12 looks like a straightforward demand: 'Continue to work out your salvation with fear and trembling.' We might put it this way: 'Work hard at being a Christian!' Good advice! – but how can I do it? Where will I get the will and the power? The next verse has the answer. God is at work! 'For it is God who works in you to will and to act according to his good purpose.' There you see the principle. God is at work – join Him! And real Christians do join Him. That is part of the evidence that God is at work.

Here are some more examples. In Romans, Paul commands, '*Yield* yourselves unto God!' (*Romans 6:13*, KJV). There is that word 'yield'. But how? In the next verse Paul shows us that God is at work. 'For sin shall not be your master' (*Romans 6:14*). If that depended mainly on me, Paul could not be so certain. Again:

> Just as you used to offer the parts of your body in slavery to impurity and to ever-increasing wickedness, so now offer them in slavery to righteousness leading to holiness. (*Romans 6:19*)

What hope is there that I can do that? Verse 22 has the answer:

> But now that you have been set free from sin and have become slaves to God, the benefit you reap leads to holiness, and the result is eternal life. (*Romans 6:22*)

Look what God has done! He has set His people free from sin!

Other books of the New Testament bear out the same truth. In 1 Thessalonians 2:12 Paul urges Christians 'to live lives worthy of God, who calls you into his kingdom and glory.' That is a fine goal, but will we do it? Paul thought we would. He had no great confidence in men without God. But God, through His word, will prevail. Paul follows up his admonition by speaking of 'the word of God, which is at work in you who believe' (*1 Thessalonians 2:13*). That is where his confidence lay.

Sometimes Paul does not give a command at all. God is at work, and that is that!

> Now about brotherly love we do not need to write to you, for you yourselves have been taught by God to love each other. And in fact, you do love all the brothers throughout Macedonia. (*1 Thessalonians 4:9–10*)

That is quite a statement! But now Paul adds, 'Yet we urge you, brothers, to do so more and more.' God is at work – join Him!

All prayer for Christians in the New Testament starts with this basic idea: God is at work. Here is how Paul prayed for the Thessalonians:

We constantly pray for you, that our God may count you worthy of his calling, and that by his power he may fulfil every good purpose of yours and every act prompted by your faith. (*2 Thessalonians 1:11*)

Who will fulfil 'every good purpose' and 'every act?' The Thessalonian Christians? Not according to Paul. It was their business to fall in with God's work. *But God would do it*.

Listen to Paul as he describes how he prays for the Philippians:

And this is my prayer: that your love may abound more and more in knowledge and depth of insight, so that you may be able to discern what is best and may be pure and blameless until the day of Christ, filled with the fruit of righteousness that comes through Jesus Christ – to the glory and praise of God. (*Philippians 1:9–11*)

That is a large prayer. Would it be done? Here is Paul's answer from verse 6: 'He who began a good work in you will carry it on to completion until the day of Christ Jesus.' Paul's confidence was in the work of God!

Because God is at work in His people, we meet some strange verses in Scripture. For example: 'Consider it pure joy, my brothers, whenever you face trials of many kinds' (*James 1:2*). Pure joy? There is no joy in the prospect of failing and falling. This verse makes sense only if God is already powerfully at work. And James was sure that He was at work. In the next verse he says, 'You know that the testing of your faith develops perseverance.' And how could we know that? Not by trusting ourselves in temptation. But we may put our confidence where James had his, in God!

What is wrong with Christians? In part, the answer is: they have been discouraged. Should they stay that way? That depends on whom you ask. Here a conference tells them: 'You are in need of the victorious Christian life.' There a pastor says: 'You're carnal, that is your problem.' Elsewhere an author writes: 'You are not abiding in Christ.' If all these things are characteristically true of them, believers ought to be downcast.

But let us ask God's word. 'My sheep listen to my voice,' says Jesus, ' . . . and they follow me' (*John 10:27*). 'You have been set free from sin,' says Paul in Romans 6:22. 'We see in you "things that accompany salvation,"' says the writer of Hebrews 6:9. 'You, dear children, are from God and have overcome [false spirits],' John says in 1 John 4:4. Why? '*Because the one who is in you is greater than the one who is in the world.*' Christian, take heart!

8: *The Sufficiency of Christ*

The claim that there are two kinds of Christians has led to a tragedy: Christians have been made discouraged without cause. And the same teaching has done even more serious harm. It has led to the denial that Christ is all the believer needs. To seek something beyond Christ is heresy. Yet I, along with countless others, have done just that.

Let me paint you a picture. Correct me if I am wrong. But think about what I say. No one, that I know of, would knowingly play a part in the picture I am about to sketch. But the practical effect of a great amount of our teaching adds up to this:

1. A man stands to preach to Christians. His text is taken from God's Word. It contains some command.
2. The preacher speaks to his hearers as Christians. He commends them for being believers.
3. He takes the command from the Scriptures as typical of things his hearers habitually fail to do. Why do they fail? They need the power of the Spirit, a power available to all Christians. *He tells them that they do not show that power.*
4. 'Being justified,' he says in effect, 'is a wonderful thing. It gets you through the door. But it is nothing compared to the "yielded", "spiritual", "victorious" life yet awaiting you.' With those words, Christ is put in second place.

These is no intention on the part of the speaker to downgrade the Lord Jesus. I do not mean to imply that there is. I am speaking, not of what he intends to do, but of what he does. 'Receiving Christ is nothing; being 'Spirit-filled' is everything!' In effect, that is said thousands of times a week from our pulpits, and the speakers themselves do not know that they are saying it. They would deny it vehemently!

Of course, the whole contrast is wrong. When I received Christ, I received the One of whom Paul said:

> In Christ *all the fulness of the Deity lives* in bodily form, and you have been given fulness in Christ, who is the head over every power and authority. (*Colossians 2:9–10*)

God's glorious secret is: 'Christ in you, the hope of glory' (*Colossians 1:27*). 'We proclaim him,' Paul adds in the following verse, '. . . so that we may present everyone perfect in Christ.' Paul's main emphasis, even to believers, was not the Holy Spirit. He preached Christ! In fact, any contrast between Christ's work in the believer and the work of the Spirit in the believer would have seemed utterly foreign to Paul. To him, the Spirit was 'the Spirit of Christ' (*Romans 8:9*). And that Spirit controls or fills every believer. Look at the whole verse:

> You, however, are controlled not by the sinful nature but by the Spirit, if the Spirit of God lives in you. And if anyone does not have the Spirit of Christ, he does not belong to Christ.

If anyone belongs to Christ, he is controlled or filled by the Spirit.

Paul's 'Christ' brings the fulness of God to each believer when He comes. And He brings all else. Christ, Paul tells us, 'has become for us wisdom from God – that is, our righteousness, holiness and redemption' (*1 Corinthians 1:30*). That is why 'it is written: Let him who boasts boast in the Lord' (*1 Corinthians 1:31*). No wonder Christ is 'the hope of glory'!

Christ is sufficient. That is the theme of the New Testament. The Lord Jesus is so intimately related to both Father and Spirit, that to receive Him is also to receive the Father and the Spirit. 'Whoever accepts me,' Jesus said, 'accepts the one who sent me' (*John 13:20*). All that we need Christ brings with Him. In beginning with the Son, we begin with the Father and the Spirit as well. All are ours in Christ!

'But wait,' someone says. 'No Christian is as wise as he should be, nor as dedicated, nor as free from sin. Doesn't that prove that something more is needed?' Not at all! It simply proves what the word 'growth' implies. It proves that Christ gives out His good things over a lifetime.

I do not need something else or more than Christ. All I need is the *same*, all-sufficient relationship to last, and to deepen, and to grow, for the rest of my days. I need to grow in 'the grace and knowledge of our Lord and Saviour Jesus Christ' (*2 Peter 3:18*). And I shall do so, and so shall you – though in differing degrees – if we are Christians. Why? Because 'he who began a good work in you will carry it on to completion' (*Philippians 1:6*). And how long will He do that? 'Until the day of Jesus Christ!'

The letter to the Galatians is about seeking for 'something more' than Christ. There Paul attacks men who look in the law for 'something more.' The same principle, however, applies to us if we look anywhere for something beyond the Lord Jesus. In Galatians Paul curses those who urge Christians to look beyond Christ. We must beware that we do not fall under that curse!

Let us take a look at Galatians. Even before Paul states the problem, he gets in a blow. He describes Christ as the One 'who gave himself for our sins to rescue us from the present evil age' (*Galatians 1:4*). It is the will of God that

Christ should do it, and not another. Then Paul describes the problem:

> I am astonished that you are so quickly deserting the one who called you by the grace of Christ and are turning to a different gospel. (*1:6*)

What did you call that, Paul? 'A different gospel!' – what a name for teaching that says, 'Christ is fine, as far as He goes, but you need "more".' Paul says of the man who teaches such a thing, 'Let him be eternally condemned' (*1:8*).

In Galatians 2:20 Paul shows the source of his power to live for God. 'Christ,' he says, 'lives in me.' The same Christ 'who loved me and gave himself for me.' Christ had lived in Paul, in this same way, since the day Paul came to Him. Paul is not discussing some special experience that most others did not have. How often we have heard this verse quoted as though it described a distinct plateau that many believers never reach! That is not Paul's point at all! Paul is telling us that he is content with Christ, the same Saviour that he shares with all other Christians. He looks for nothing beyond Christ. Christ is sufficient for Paul. And Christ is all the Galatians need.

In the third chapter Paul describes life with Christ in another way. It is life 'with the Spirit' (*3:3*). Paul and the Galatians began with Christ. But now he calls that same beginning a 'beginning with the Spirit.' Paul is not confused. When they received Christ they received the Spirit. 'Be content,' Paul seems to say, 'with what you have in Christ.' That does not mean to be content with *what we are*. Paul would never say that! No, we must be content with *what we have*. It is not what we are, however godly we may be, that holds out hope for our future. It is what we have in our Saviour, what we have in Jesus Christ.

And what we have is this: a Saviour who brings all else with Him. He is not reluctant to give us what we need. There is no secret formula, no special phrase and no unusual posture in prayer that will extort what we need from Him. As we wrestle against sin, Christ will give us the strength to live a characteristically godly life.

This subject, the sufficiency of Christ, is so important that Paul keeps pressing the issue. He has made his point, but he does not quit. He does not turn to other things. It must come home to us. Christ – the Christ we received when we were saved – is all we need. Let us trust Him and take heart!

Paul shows this in yet another way. God has made each Christian an heir with Christ (*4:7*). Do we think of an heir as a man who may get something someday? That is not Paul's view. An earthly heir may get *something*. An heir of God will surely get *all* that God has for him! As Peter put it elsewhere, Believers have 'an inheritance that can never perish, spoil or fade – kept in heaven for' them (*1 Peter 1:4*). It is true that the full inheritance will not come into our hands in this life. But the portion we need to live a godly life is already ours. We have God's Spirit. 'Because you are sons, God sent the Spirit of his Son into our hearts' (*4:6*). The Holy Spirit lives in us. But to keep the emphasis on Christ, Paul calls the Spirit, 'the Spirit of his Son.'

What thrilled Paul? Not his conscious experience, but Christ! The Galatians were in danger of getting away from Christ. So Paul pounds away at this theme: Christ, Christ, Christ! Someone might say, 'Paul, you are mad. Don't you know that no Christian will get far from the doctrine of Christ?' Paul would reply, 'It is not my business to say whether this man or that woman is a Christian. The Lord knows who are His. My job is to preach and to teach. Here is a church that is drifting into "something more". There *is* nothing "more"! I must tell them about the Lord Jesus Christ!'

With that in mind we are not surprised to see how Paul ends this letter. In thinking on the Lord Jesus, Paul has been moved to an emotional peak. 'God forbid,' he cries, 'God forbid that I should glory, save in the cross of our Lord Jesus Christ!' (*6:14*, KJV). 'Whatever you Galatians do,' I think I hear him say, 'I must find my *all* in Jesus Christ!'

Paul was not alone in the way he exalted Christ. He was taught by the Spirit to follow the example of Christ Himself. On the night before His death Jesus spoke of the coming Spirit:

> [The Spirit] will bring glory to me by taking from what is mine and making it known to you. All that belongs to the Father is mine. That is why I said the Spirit will take from what is mine and make it known to you. (*John 16:14–15*)

Why do men come to Christ? Is it to know more of the Spirit? That is not the first thing. The work of the Spirit is to lead men to a better appreciation of Christ. To make an experience with the Spirit a step beyond Christ is to miss the point. 'He will bring glory to me,' Jesus said. There is no knowledge higher than the knowledge of Christ.

And the knowledge of Christ is *practical* knowledge. We may think that a 'victorious life' needs more than the Saviour that we first met. But listen to this:

> For everyone born of God has overcome the world. This is the victory that has overcome the world, even our faith. Who is it that overcomes the world? Only he who believes that Jesus is the Son of God. (*1 John 5:4–5*)

Should any man aim higher than to 'overcome the world'? Judge for yourself! Yet it is the simple believer who wins this victory. It is 'everyone born of God', without exception. Why? Because when he believes in Jesus Christ, all that God has is his.

When we turn to the letter to the Hebrews we see the same thing. Jesus Christ is the practical answer to the believer's needs. For example, he needs holiness. 'Without holiness no one will see the Lord' (*Hebrews 12:14*). Where will he get it? Through something beyond Christ? Not at all! God will provide it through the Lord Jesus. It is as good as done! By the death of Christ, God has made a new covenant with His people. In it God says, 'I will put my laws in their hearts, and I will write them on their minds' (*Hebrews 10:16*). In other words God will teach His own to be obedient. They will keep His laws. God Himself will see to it. That is the reason why the writer can end his book with this confident prayer:

> May the God of peace, who through the blood of the eternal covenant brought back from the dead our Lord Jesus, that great Shepherd of the sheep, equip you with everything good for doing his will, and may he work in us what is pleasing to him, through Jesus Christ, to whom be glory for ever and ever. Amen. (*Hebrews 13:20–21*)

This great work is done 'through Jesus Christ.' Christ is all we need.

Let me close this chapter by suggesting a difficulty. Someone may ask, 'What is the use, then, of all the exhortations and warnings in the Bible? If Christ, as we first received Him, is all we need, what is the point of the commands to live a godly life? Won't that take care of itself? If God guarantees my progress, why make my own effort?' These are natural questions. Let me see if I can answer them.

We must keep in mind that we are not mechanical

beings and God does not treat us men like machines. That is important for two reasons. First, it shows us why we do not all progress at the same rate. It is true that God leads His people toward the goals He has in mind. That means that we shall surely move forward over the course of our Christian lives. But God's means in doing this are the means one person uses to influence another. He uses such things as persuasion and discipline to lead us along. This is not done mechanically. It leaves us with a part to play in responding to His persuasion and in profiting by His discipline. Our progress is assured because we are new creatures and because the Holy Spirit lives within us. This means that, generally speaking, we will want to do what God desires. But we are always in a position where we have to be responsive to what God is doing. We are not robots; we are living, breathing men and women.

Second, this helps us see the place of commands in God's programme. God uses commands as one means to get His work done. If that seems hard to grasp, this story from Acts 27 should help. A fierce storm has come down upon Paul and his shipmates as he is being taken, a prisoner, to Rome. It seems likely that all on board will be drowned.

But God shows Paul otherwise. And Paul passes along the good news to the sailors:

> But now I urge you to keep up your courage, because not one of you will be lost; only the ship will be destroyed. Last night an angel of the God whose I am and whom I serve stood beside me and said, 'Do not be afraid, Paul. You must stand trial before Caesar; and God has graciously given you the lives of all who sail with you.' (*Acts 27:22–24*)

God said they would live. That was that! Paul adds, 'I have faith in God that it will happen just as he told me' (*Acts 27:25*). No doubt about it!

The story goes on. Some seamen do not believe Paul. They start to lower a boat to row to land. Now watch what happens. Paul speaks up and says to the soldiers, 'Unless these men stay with the ship, you cannot be saved' (*Acts 27:31*). What? Didn't God say that all lives would be saved? Yes, and it was certain! But it was not automatic. God would not do it mechanically. He was dealing with men, not with machines. It would be done. All would be saved. But it would be done in God's way. It would be done through His word to Paul. So the soldiers cut the ropes of the boat being lowered. The boat fell away. A shipwreck followed. But God kept His word and all lived to reach the island of Malta!

We need God's warnings and God's commands. He carries out His will in us through them. We dare not lay them aside. But the overall outcome is sure. When a man receives Jesus Christ, he receives the One who brings all else with Him. The believer needs nothing beyond the Lord Jesus and His word. With Christ came the fulness of God:

> For in Christ all the fulness of the Deity lives in bodily form, and you have been given fulness in Christ, who is the head over every power and authority. (*Colossians 2:9–10*)

To seek something more than Christ is heresy.

Are you seeking 'something more' than the Saviour? Maybe you are dissatisfied with yourself. Have you let that dissatisfaction extend to Him? Have you said, 'If I just had something more than Jesus Christ'? If so, go to Him and tell Him. Repent of that sin, as many of us have had to do. Worship the Saviour, even as you wrestle against sin.

Where shall we go if the battle is too heavy for us? Here is Jesus' answer:

> Come to me, all you who are weary and burdened, and I will give you rest. Take my yoke upon you and learn from

me, for I am gentle and humble in heart, and you will find rest for your souls. For my yoke is easy and my burden is light. (*Matthew 11:28–30*)

Jesus directed men to Himself. It is true, He gives them a 'yoke' when they come. All is not a breeze for the Christian. But His 'yoke is easy.' Why? Because He shares it with us. That means, as Matthew Henry once wrote, 'His yoke is lined with love!'

9: *The Sins of the Christian*

If you have followed me thus far, you may have wondered how to put together two things I have said. On the one hand, I have insisted that God is at work in His people. His work makes each of them characteristically righteous. On the other hand, I have said that God's people sin daily. Can these things both be true?

They are both true. To understand how they are true will also explain why spiritual Christians can be told that they are carnal, and be made to believe it. I think you will soon understand why preachers and teachers can easily discourage godly men and women.

First, you must get a firm grip on one fact. It is a fact that we who preach have often failed to emphasise: Christians and non-Christians are utterly different. We often miss this, and we draw the line in the wrong place. We may put a fine line between the 'saved' man and the 'unsaved' man. We may say that they may be practically alike. God never said that, but I have. Then we may draw a great gulf between one saved man and another. 'This Christian is merely saved,' we may say. 'But that believer is Spirit-filled.' And in saying that, we put the 'great gulf' in the wrong place.

How are believers and unbelievers utterly different? In this way: a Christian often pleases God; a non-Christian has never yet done so. In other words, everything that an unbeliever does is sin – everything, without exception!

If you are not a child of God, you have never yet done

one thing that has pleased God. Nothing! You have gone to church, sung the hymns, and given your money. Yet it was all sin. Every bit of it! God has plainly told you so, in His word.

Let me show you what God has said. You would not want to take my word for it. Here is how God describes the unrenewed mind:

> The mind of sinful man is death . . . because the sinful mind is hostile to God. It does not submit to God's law, nor can it do so. Those controlled by the sinful nature cannot please God. (*Romans 8:6–8*)

The Lord says three things here:

1. The unrenewed man is an enemy of God.
2. The unrenewed mind cannot be brought into line with God's law. Therefore,
3. The unrenewed man can never please God.

We may put this another way. The unrenewed man never exercises true faith in God. He believes in himself. Why should he lean on another? But the letter to the Hebrews tells us, 'Without faith it is impossible to please God' (*Hebrews 11:6*). Paul is even more explicit: 'Everything that does not come from faith is sin' (*Romans 14:23*). If the non-Christian is an enemy of God, as God plainly says, it is not surprising that he never puts his faith in his enemy. If he had faith in God his hostility would be gone.

Paul once wrote of the unconverted world, 'There is no one who does good, not even one' (*Romans 3:12*). But don't our eyes tell us otherwise? Don't we see unsaved men do good things every day? How can this be?

The answer is not hard to find. For an act to be good, it must arise from good motives. And one of those motives must be the glory of God. Where that motive is missing, every act has a fatal flaw. An unsaved man may have some good motives in what he does. That is, he may do something for the sake of others. That is fine, *as far as it goes*. We do not want to deny that. But it does not go far enough. God commands, 'Whether you eat or drink or whatever you do, do it all for the glory of God' (*1 Corinthians 10:31*). But each thing the unbeliever does breaks this command. For that reason, he never once pleases God.

You must not get the idea that godliness mainly consists in doing things that the world never does, and *vice versa*. Sometimes it is so. There are some things that the world does that the Christian must not do. But the great mass of things that the unsaved man does, the believer does also. Both eat; both sleep; both go to work. Both read the newspaper; both wash, and both write. These things take up the majority of men's lives. Their differences are not primarily found in what they do. They differ in why they do them. One does all that he does without seeking to bring glory or praise to God. The other does what he does to please and magnify the Lord. And the difference is 'all the difference in the world.'

One man is alive to God, and he expresses that life. The other is only alive to this world, and he expresses that life. The difference is not incidental. It is basic.

Why do we call a sinning Christian a 'godly man'? Not because we condone sin. Not because we think it is a trifle. Not that at all! We call a sinning believer a godly man because we must always try to give men names or titles that characterise them. We do not call an unsaved man 'a sinner' because he occasionally sins. We call him a sinner because that is what characterises his life. As we have seen, his every act is sinful. But a godly man is characterised by righteous motives and godly acts. So we call him a godly man even though some of his motives and deeds are sinful.

Our sins are many. God help us never to rest content with even one sin! Let us long to be delivered from all iniquity. Let us hunger and thirst for righteousness. Perfection is our goal. No other goal is worthy of the Christian.

Our sins are many. That is why it is so easy to discourage the Christian. Tell him that he is carnal, and his heart reminds him how often he fails. Tell him he does not love God as he should, and he knows that it is so. Tell him that he does not long after a lost world as he ought. He knows it, perhaps better than the preacher does. Is it easy to discourage him? Yes, very easy. Keep him looking at himself. Require him constantly to take his spiritual temperature. You will discourage him in no time.

Many seem to have the idea that as a man grows in holiness he will feel more holy. I do not think he will. But leave that notion around where Christians can trip over it, and they will. You can easily get men to expect to feel more holy as they progress in their Christian lives. But in a true believer that idea will lead to discouragement. Why? Because growth in holiness will lead a man to see more and more of his own sinfulness.

The unsaved man feels nothing of sinfulness. He may hate the results of sin in his life. He may despise what it does to his family. He may rue the fact that he does not live up to his own standards. But he would remain content to have all his sins if they would not bear such bitter fruit.

Not so with the Christian! He hates sin. His is a lifelong repentance. He longs not to grieve his Lord. So his sin is a greater grief to him each day. *He does not feel more holy.* Instead, he stands on the Word of God. God is at work in him; that is his hope. Not what he is, but what God is doing! In other words, his hope is in God Himself.

What a terrible thing it must be, then, to rob the believer of God's promises! Leave him to himself and you can tear the heart out of him. Keep telling him how much he could do, *if* he were only what he ought to be. At last you will drive him to despair. It is only the goodness of God that will keep him from utter depression. Somehow, thank the Lord, Christians do survive, even under that kind of treatment. They still have their Bibles. They still may read, 'Christ in you, the hope of glory!'

Because our sins are many, God has provided a great forgiveness. He has given us a general cry for pardon: 'Forgive us our debts, as we also have forgiven our debtors (*Matthew 6:12*). But someone may say, 'Don't make a general confession. Name your sins.' Of course we must not try to hide any known sin from God. How foolish! God knows all. We may fool ourselves; we cannot deceive Him. I thank Him, however, for this privilege: I may pray, 'Forgive me all my sins, Lord!' with confidence. God knew what He was doing when he gave us that prayer. I do not know all my sins. The Psalmist asked, 'Who can discern his errors?' and added, 'Forgive my hidden faults' (*Psalm 19:12*). I trust God's forgiveness, because I know His grace. 'Where sin increased, grace increased all the more' (*Romans 5:20*). Through the mercy of God, increasing sin meets increasing grace. Hallelujah, what a Saviour!

But what if I become proud, and lose my penitent attitude, what then? Then things will change. They will change because the Lord will not leave one of His own in that condition. If I am a child of God He will go to work to bring me back to my knees. How? God has his ways! He is not at a loss with His children as I may be with mine. He may open my eyes from His Word. He may send unpleasant circumstances. Or He may send some unexpected blessing that will throw light on my ingratitude. God knows what to do.

What if I do not respond? If I can go on in unforgiven sin – if I can continue in impenitence – then I must question whether I am a child of God. It makes no difference that I preach and write books. It makes no difference that I have 'assurance'. My 'assurance' is a lie. Listen to Scripture:

> If we deliberately keep on sinning after we have received the knowledge of the truth, no sacrifice for sins is left, but only a fearful expectation of judgment and of raging fire that will consume the enemies of God. (*Hebrews 10:26–27*)

If I am content to go on in sin, I am an enemy, an adversary of God. Hell, not heaven, follows at the end of my life. I must not comfort myself in this state. I must repent!

But for God's people there is comfort. God is at work in them. He has given His people new hearts. They are not yet perfect, but their hearts are inclined toward God. God made them that way. He has done what He said He would do:

> This is the covenant I will make with them after that time, says the Lord. I will put my laws in their hearts, and I will write them on their minds . . . Their sins and lawless acts I will remember no more. (*Hebrews 10:16–17*)

God is at work in His people!

Here is another truth, full of comfort: God *has been* at work in His people. All along! Perhaps you have been one of the discouraged ones. Maybe you have felt defeated. Are those years of discouragment lost? Not at all! If you are a child of God, He has been at work in you. Like a child, you were misinformed. But it is more common to misinform a youngster than to stunt his growth. Those years are not lost. They felt wasted. They looked lost. But feelings mean little. I repeat: God *has been* at work in His people. Christian, take heart!

Let me close this chapter by speaking as a teacher to other teachers. All of us teach someone, so I am speaking to us all. First, let us pray that God will keep us from discouraging His saints. We need prayer for this. We must never discourage the children of God.

Second, let us keep preaching the gospel to one another. The gospel is 'the power of God' for salvation (*Romans 1:16*). Let us not assume that because a man has made a profession of faith he is necessarily a believer. Let us not omit the gospel in dealing with all, including our own children. We cannot injure our brother by telling him the good news. We cannot do him harm by urging him to hate sin and to love righteousness. Let us enter into the spirit of Paul, who preached Christ, 'admonishing and teaching everyone with all wisdom, so that we may present everyone perfect in Christ' (*Colossians 1:28*).

10: *The Christian and his Teachers*

Thus far I have been very hard on those of us who teach. I have traced up the discouragement among Christians to our teaching and preaching. I have said that, in effect, we teachers have denied that God is at work in all of His children. We did not mean to deny it. But that was what we implied when we insisted that there are two kinds of Christians.

Now I must warn you of a danger. It is this. You must not conclude that you do not need teachers. I fear someone may say, 'Well, just give me my Bible, then, and I'll study on my own. I don't need the help of anyone.' For two reasons, that is a grave mistake. First, the Bible shows plainly that you need to be taught by others. Second, history amply bears out that need.

Let us heed what the Bible says. Do you remember the list of gifts at the end of 1 Corinthians 12. This is how it starts: 'In the church God has appointed first of all apostles, second prophets, third teachers . . .' (*1 Corinthians 12:28*).

Who were these people? 'First apostles' – an apostle was a kind of teacher. Paul is a good example of an apostle. His great work was preaching and teaching. The other apostles did the same thing. They taught.

'Second prophets' – in both Testaments prophets were teachers. The content of their teaching might vary. One might give a prediction, another a warning. In either case, the prophet taught.

'Third teachers' – their name shows what they did. They taught. In the churches of the First Century the Holy Spirit placed three types of men who taught.

God does not waste effort. He put teachers in the church because His people need teachers. You need teachers; so do I. God put teachers first in order, because His children need teaching more than anything else that man can do. We must not neglect teaching; we must not despise teachers. 'The elders who direct the affairs of the church well are worthy of double honour,' Paul wrote, 'especially those whose work is preaching and teaching' (*I Timothy 5:17*). Church leaders are to be respected, especially those who work at teaching. That is the command of God.

History confirms our need for teachers. We soon learn that we need the good things that God has shown to men who lived before us. The early church had the Bible, but it could not look back on the ministry of centuries of gifted men who had known and used the New Testament. So the early church struggled to define such questions as the nature of God and of Christ. The truth they sought was in the Bible. God chose, however, to make it plain to the church over hundreds of years. The nature of God was repeatedly discussed by the church's teachers. They searched the Scriptures for answers to their questions. Eventually they came to see what the Word of God taught. After much debate they reached a consensus. They had no authority from God to impose their understanding on the church. But generations of Christians have examined the Scriptures for themselves and have decided that these early teachers were correct in their understanding. Each generation has benefited from the work of these men. We are the heirs of these teachers who have gone before us.

During many centuries much of the church lost its grip on the doctrine of justification by faith. That doctrine says that God makes men right with Himself when they trust in

Jesus Christ. Faith has always been God's way. Each man saved, has been saved through faith. There is no other path to God. Still, as clear as this is to us today, it took the sixteenth-century Reformation to make it widely understood. Teachers like Martin Luther and John Calvin trumpeted it forth. Before their time men trusted Christ and were saved. They felt they were Christ's (and they were). Yet most Christians would have been hard pressed to give a plain account of how they were converted. God used the teachers of the Reformation to clarify the doctrine of Scripture. One important result: more and more believers were able to enjoy the assurance that they were right with God.

The last one hundred years or more has seen a re-emphasis on the return of Christ. He will come personally, visibly. That was always taught in the Bible. Yet, for many, it had fallen into the shadows. But now teachers are pressing the importance of this fact on men everywhere. And they hear in response the cry: 'Come, Lord Jesus!'

We need living teachers. We need the help of men who have commented on the Scriptures in days gone by. Charles Spurgeon, a preacher of the nineteenth century, spoke wisely when he said to his ministerial students:

> Of course, you are not such wiseacres as to think or say that you can expound Scripture without assistance from the works of divines and learned men who have laboured before you . . . It seems odd, that certain men who talk so much of what the Holy Spirit reveals to themselves, should think so little of what he has revealed to others . . . A respectable acquaintance with the opinions of the giants of the past, might have saved many an erratic thinker from wild interpretations and outrageous inferences. (*Commenting And Commentaries*, Grand Rapids, 1954, p. 1)

Let me add this. We must always be wary of men who preach their experience and claim to be above theological education. Have you heard this saying, 'A man with an experience is never at the mercy of a man with a doctrine.' That statement ought to send a chill up your spine. In plain words it often means, 'No one can teach me anything – not even from the Bible!' But what does God say? 'To the law and to the testimony! If they do not speak according to this word [no matter how great their experience], they have no light . . .' (*Isaiah 8:20*). Education at the feet of godly men is a great gift from God. Some of us have not had as much of it as we would have liked. We need teachers, men who themselves have felt the need to be taught. Both the Bible and history tell us so plainly.

Our teachers, of course, are mere men. They are not gods. We must check what they say by the light of God's Word. We need their suggestions, their hints, and their guidance. But we must catch the spirit of the Bereans. Luke wrote of them:

> Now the Bereans were of more noble character than the Thessalonians, for they received the message with great eagerness and examined the Scriptures every day to see if what Paul said was true. (*Acts 17:11*)

May we do the same!

Because God's people need teachers, teachers bear a great weight of responsibility. We have not thought of that often enough. No wonder God has said, 'Not many of you should presume to be teachers, my brothers . . .' (*James 3:1*). Those are sobering words. Again, God has said of an elder, 'He must not be a recent convert, or he may become conceited and fall under the same judgment as the devil' (*1 Timothy 3:6*). May God help those of us who teach!

Paul writes about the quality of our teaching in 1 Corinthians 3:9–15. We need to look at this passage for two reasons. First, it has been widely misunderstood. These verses have been used to prove that a Christian man or woman may be carnal throughout life. That is a wrong use of this section. In the second place, this passage is a solemn warning to all of us to examine what we teach. Here are verses 9–11:

> You are . . . God's building. By the grace God has given me, I laid a foundation as an expert builder, and someone else is building on it. But each one should be careful how he builds. For no-one can lay any foundation other than the one already laid, which is Jesus Christ.

Paul is a teacher. The church is like a house. Paul has laid the foundation of the Corinthian church. That foundation is Christ. No other foundation will do. Other teachers follow Paul. Let each be careful how he builds.

Paul continues in verses 12–13:

> If any man builds on this foundation using gold, silver, costly stones, wood, hay or straw, his work will be shown for what it is, because the Day will bring it to light. It will be revealed with fire, and the fire will test the quality of each man's work.

Note this carefully: Paul is not writing about the 'works' of believers. He is talking about a single 'work', the work of teaching. There is such a thing as good teaching. He likens good teaching, or its results, to precious metals and costly building materials. There is poor teaching also. He compares poor teaching, or its results, to wood, hay and straw. At 'the Day', the building will be tried by fire to test the quality of the teaching.

Finally let us look at verses 14–15:

If what he has built survives, he will receive his reward. If it is burned up, he will suffer loss; he himself will be saved, but only as one escaping through the flames.

Every man's *teaching* will be tested. If it is good teaching, its results will abide. If it is poor teaching, its results will not survive. Yet the teacher himself will be saved.

We must not suppose that all our teaching is of the same quality. We aim at truth. We fall short. We come short in differing degrees. So we will be rewarded for our teaching in differing degrees, in keeping with what we have taught.

Let me use myself as an illustration. Since I was drawn to Christ many years ago, I have grown. As a child of God I have the Holy Spirit at work in me. I trust I know the Saviour better than I knew Him fifteen or twenty years ago. During that time I have taught God's church. I see now that a part of what I taught was not true. All my 'untruth' may have seemed to build up the church. It may have brought new members. It may have produced activity and programmes. It may have excited my people.

Untrue teaching may sound good, but it will not abide the fire. It will be burned up. Men that I thought I had brought to Christ may not survive the judgment. Yet I, if I am a genuine believer, will be saved. I may be a godly man. I may be living for the Lord. I certainly will be, if I am a Christian. But I must realise that all this will not keep me from teaching some error. I must cry out with the Psalmist, 'Open my eyes that I may see wonderful things in your law' (*Psalm 119:18*). I am utterly cast on God. I must pray again, 'Let me understand the teaching of your precepts . . .' (*Psalm 119:27*).

Some men think it is a small matter whose teaching they sit under. 'He is a good man,' they say. 'He is a man with leadership ability.' Or, 'He is a great speaker, I could listen to him by the hour.' Or again, 'My children like it there. That's important to me.' All of those things may be true, and much more. But here is the acid test: is the teaching carefully and painstakingly true to the word of God? That is *the* question. Does the preacher exalt the work of God in the soul? Is Christ the all-*sufficient* Saviour in his eyes. Or is there much 'more' beyond Him? I warn you: these questions are nearer to the heart of God than all the eloquence or leadership ability or appeal to young people, in the world.

The Word of God is the only test. So often other tests are applied by godly men. 'Will it fill the church?' is a very common one.

I myself was fooled by it for many years. Some men professed to be unconcerned with numbers. They seemed as content to reach one man as to reach fifty. I could not agree with that. Christ died for 'numbers', a great number of individuals. I felt that I had to be concerned with 'numbers'. But I had to learn not to measure my success by the number of converts. I must preach. I must pray. God, however, must give the success. As Paul said, 'I planted the seed, Apollos watered it, but God made it grow' (*1 Corinthians 3:6*).

'But,' I hear someone say, 'there will always be an increase, won't there? The church will grow, won't it? So that is a test, isn't it?' Let me answer with a word God gave Isaiah.

> So is my word that goes out from my mouth. It will not return to me empty, but will accomplish what I desire and achieve the purpose for which I sent it. (*Isaiah 55:11*)

God says plainly that the preaching of His Word will *always* accomplish what He pleases. The Word of God is *always* successful.

Does that mean that each faithful preacher will be able to build a large church? Hardly! Isaiah was a faithful preacher, but he watched godliness decline before his eyes.

Or take Jeremiah. He was a faithful preacher. Yet he saw so few turn to God that he was almost driven to despair. He wanted to quit, but he could not do it. Listen to him.

> But if I say, 'I will not mention him or speak any more in his name,' his word is in my heart like a burning fire, shut up in my bones. I am weary of holding it in; indeed I cannot. (*Jeremiah 20:9*)

God did what He pleased through the preaching of Isaiah and Jeremiah, but they had little *visible* fruit to show for it.

So it may be with us. One man may see a great harvest of souls. Thank God! Another may see a small crop. Thank God again! Still another may see no harvest at all. Thank God for that also! In every case God will honour His word. In every case it will do what He wants it to do. He is doing a thousand things through His word. We must not limit Him to one, the reaping of souls.

This was a hard lesson for me to learn. With many others I had the presumption to say, 'The only reason God has left you on earth is to win souls.' Look at the omniscience in that statement. Am I God, that I can know all His purposes? Has He told me all that He is doing? Isn't it just possible that He had something else He wanted to do in His people before He took them home? Am I infallible, that no one would dare challenge my statement?

God is free to be God! One man says, 'God must save'. Another insists, 'God must heal'. Still another claims, 'God must bless our mission programme'. But all are wrong. God will do what He has said He will do. All will turn out according to His promise in the end. But in any individual case we do not know what He plans. He retains His freedom to be God.

If we are content for God to be God, it will save us from many errors. I remember how I used to whip Christians verbally. I had a soul-winning programme. God was going to bless it, or else! But He was not necessarily in my programme. My people did not respond as I thought they should. So, what did I do? I preached soul-winning. I taught soul-winning. I urged soul-winning. I acted as if my little scheme for saving men was the latest word from the Lord.

Certainly there is nothing wrong in wanting to see men come to Christ. There is everything right about it. But my emphasis was on 'seeing' them come. I did not like to let God work. I wanted to 'see' results. Yet the hesitancy of my godly people should have taught me caution. On the average, because God is at work in His people, they should have responded. Instead, they went on with their own witness, while I had to work at keeping them feeling guilty to keep them active in my programme.

The lessons here are these. First, God's people need teachers, men who will stay near to the Word of God. Second, God's teachers need His people. If teachers will look closely they will find that God is at work in His own. Third, the Christian and his teacher are a team. They are more than that; they are parts of the same body. They are interdependent. They work together in Christ. That is their satisfying task and privilege. Christian, take heart!

11 : *Getting a Grasp of the Bible*

I fear I preached for many years before I knew what the Bible was about. Yet what I am going to tell you will look so simple and obvious that you will wonder why I want to devote a chapter to it. No-one – at least, no Christian – will argue with what I am about to say. But stay with me. Here is the fact that I so often overlooked:

The Bible is about God.

Did any believer ever doubt that the Bible is about God? What is so startling about that? Could any man be a preacher of the gospel and not know that? Doesn't every Christian know that the Bible is about God? Well, let us see.

For years I thought that the Bible was about man and what he ought to do. If you had listened to me you would have heard me refer to God to show you what your responsibilities were. I would say things like this. 'God made you, therefore you ought to serve Him.' Or, 'Christ died for you, so you ought to live for Him.' Or, 'Christ will return some day, so you had better be ready.'

In each case I spoke the truth. Because God made you, you ought to serve Him. Because Christ died for you, Christian, you ought to live for Him. Because Christ will return, you ought to be ready. May the Lord help me to keep preaching these truths!

The trouble, however, with a steady diet of this kind of preaching is that it soon reduces the Bible to a book about man. Of course, the Bible is about both God and man. It has its own emphasis, however, and *that emphasis is on God, and what God is doing.* It is not first of all on man and what he ought to do. A false emphasis perverts the truth. In theory we may believe that the Bible is about God while, because of our emphasis, we deny it in practice.

Something else happened when my emphasis was wrong. Not only did I talk too much about man, but I began to degrade God. Often I spoke of what God could do, *if* . . . ! *If* Christians were not so carnal, just think what God could do! *If* believers would only dedicate themselves, how quickly God could conquer the world! *If* we would only pray more, how much God could get done! Before I knew it I had made a god utterly tied up by the limits man put upon him. *But He was not the God of the Bible!*

My god could never have said what Isaiah's God said. Listen to Him again:

> [My word] will not return to me empty, but will accomplish what I desire and achieve the purpose for which I sent it. (*Isaiah 55:11*)

My little god could have sent out his word and hoped that it would accomplish what he desired. But apart from his foresight he would have had to adopt the motto: *only time will tell.* Supposedly the god of my preaching was all-powerful. Actually he was nearly as helpless as I am.

Am I exaggerating? Perhaps! Certainly if some dear friend had told me that I had a helpless god I would have laughed at him. I would have said, 'Didn't God create the universe? Don't the heavens declare His glory? Didn't He save a wretch like me? Just look,' I might have added, 'how great my God is!' But my faith and understanding fell far short of what they should have been. A story from Luke will show you what I mean.

A Roman soldier had a slave on the verge of death. He sent word by some Jewish elders to Jesus to come and to heal his slave, and the Lord Jesus agreed to go. As Jesus went the soldier had second thoughts. He said:

Lord, don't trouble yourself, for I do not deserve to have you come under my roof. That is why I did not even consider myself worthy to come to you. But say the word and my servant will be healed. For I myself am a man under authority, with soldiers under me. I tell this one, 'Go,' and he goes; and that one, 'Come,' and he comes. I say to my servant, 'Do this,' and he does it. (*Luke 7:6–8*)

Now watch Jesus' reaction:

When Jesus heard this, he was amazed at him, and turning to the crowd following him, he said, 'I tell you, I have not found such great faith even in Israel.' (*Luke 7:9*)

What was unusual about this officer's faith? What made it greater than the faith the Lord found in Israel? Not the fact that Jesus could heal. The Jewish elders thought the same thing. What, then? His great faith lay in this: he thought Jesus could do what He pleased! He thought the Lord Jesus could say to this man, or to that demon, or to a deadly disease, 'Go!' and it would go. He believed in the power of Jesus' word.

We too talk of the power of Jesus' word. Jesus was God. We quote Hebrews 4:12(KJV): 'The word of God is quick, and *powerful*!' But how powerful? Our theory may say, 'Unlimited in power!' But what if it runs up against resistance in man? What if the Word of God commands something that man is unwilling to do? What then? Can it still be true that it will 'accomplish what I desire,' as God said?

The Roman officer had no such doubts. Why should he? Wasn't he a top-sergeant of his day? Do top-sergeants run into resistance? Of course! Do top-sergeants get their way? Of course! Ask any private! All around the Roman soldier were men who believed in God's creative power. There were men who believed that Christ could heal. But the officer alone believed that Jesus could do what He pleased. The Lord called that 'great faith'!

Like every comparison, this one can be pushed too far. God is not a top-sergeant. When His word meets resistance in men He does not ride roughshod over their wills. Instead He works to change their wills. At first God implants a new nature in the elect sinner. The sinner becomes a new man. As a new man he makes choices different from those he once made. God also nurtures this new man. He disciplines this new man. He moves him in the direction He wants the man to take. He is making that new man what He wants Him to be. In other words, God *is* God in the new man He creates. It should not surprise us, then, if God's people do His will. We would be surprised if they did not.

Have we lost the sense of the greatness of God? I believe we have. Have our churches failed to preach a God that is more than *potentially* powerful? I believe they have. More than all else our churches must regain the conviction of God's greatness. We must see that the Bible is about God, the God that is at work, the God who is ever free to do as He pleases.

Our songs, I think, will bear out what I am saying. Do you listen to what Christians are singing these days? Most large cities in America have a 'gospel-music' radio station. Listen to it. What themes do you hear? The chief theme is man and his experience. What is wrong with a song about man and his experience? Nothing! There is nothing wrong with two or three or ten such songs. What they say is not wrong; it is what they leave unsaid. Our salvation, and our walk, our home in heaven, our struggles, our hopes, and our fears are all great themes for song. But the greatest theme of all is God.

It is the dearth of God-centred songs that makes an occasional one a breath of fresh air. You will miss my point, however, if you think that I am primarily interested in changing our singing habits. Not at all! Our songs are not the *cause* of our loss of the sense of God's greatness, though songs are surprisingly influential. No, our songs reflect this loss. Singing God-centred hymns is desirable, but more than that is needed. We sing what we feel, what we believe. When once we rediscover the greatness of God, we will sing it. Our song will echo our conviction.

How shall we regain this sense of the greatness of God? Let me first suggest some things that will not work. We will not regain the sense of God's greatness by constantly repeating 'God is great!' That seems plain enough, but it needs to be emphasised. Today we hear of rallies where such phrases are repeated by hundreds and even thousands of people. These people may indeed feel that God is great. But if they are to last, feelings must feed on facts. Men must know how God is great; they must grasp in what ways He is demonstrating His greatness. Phrases like 'Praise the Lord,' 'God is great,' and 'Thank you, Jesus' may convey the feelings of the moment, but the man who uses those phrases must either have facts to keep up those feelings, or he must return to the same kind of exciting meeting again and again to sustain them.

Nor will miracles suffice! The Lord Jesus said as much. Christ once looked at men who had been fed by a miracle and said,

> I tell you the truth, you are looking for me, not because you saw miraculous signs but because you ate the loaves and had your fill. (*John 6:26*)

The miracle of the feeding of the five thousand was a pointer to the greatness of God and of Christ, but they missed it. They looked for Jesus so that they could have their bellies filled again. They thought they had found the free lunch, and they wanted it repeated. Men can see the greatest miracles and miss the glory of God. What generation was ever favoured with miracles as Jesus' generation was? Yet that generation crucified the Son of God!

Some men think that what we need is a change of *method* in our preaching. One man favours preaching from a single text. Another likes a topical approach. Still another prefers expository preaching, that is, preaching from an extended portion of Scripture. Of course, all preaching must be expository in the sense of explaining Bible truth. There is no place for the book review artist, or the political commentator, in the Christian pulpit.

The method of preaching from an extended portion may look more biblical, but in itself it means little. One man may take a chapter from God's Word and preach about man from it. Another may take the same chapter and discover God.

Here is an illustration of what I mean. Some time ago I heard a sermon on Gideon. The preacher wisely drew his information from the Bible. We followed him as he led us, verse by verse, through Gideon's call to lead Israel. We saw Gideon's fear of the Midianites. We heard his cry, 'But Lord, how can I save Israel?' (*Judges 6:15*). We watched as Gideon built an altar. We eavesdropped as he twice tested God.

I could not argue with the preacher's words. They were good words, true words. No doubt I learned things about Gideon that will prove useful. Everything was as it should have been. Everything, except one thing! The story in the book of Judges is not primarily about a man named

Gideon. That story is about God. Yes, it is true that Gideon feared and wavered and tested God and finally yielded. All of that, and much more, was true of Gideon. The essential truth, however, was this. God had made up His mind to deliver Israel, and He had made up His mind that He would do it through Gideon. The story is first of all about God!

How will Christians regain the sense of God's greatness? One part of the answer must come from those of us who teach. We must help them to see the greatness of the work of God in their own souls. If most Christians are 'carnal' or 'worldly' then all our talk of the greatness of God will be lost on them. God made the universe. But if he cannot deliver His own people from the bondage of their sinfulness, it should not surprise us if they do not feel the greatness of His power.

It will do no good to say, 'God can do it, *if* they will only let Him.' I can do great things with men, if they will 'let' me. The law of God could have done great things with men if they had 'let' it. The law was good. The law was holy. But by itself it could not give men the inclination of heart to follow it. Only God could do that through Christ. Here is how Paul sums up the situation:

> For what the law was powerless to do in that it was weakened by the sinful nature, God did by sending his own Son in the likeness of sinful man to be a sin offering. And so he condemned sin in sinful man, in order that the righteous requirements of the law might be fully met in us, who do not live according to the sinful nature but according to the Spirit. (*Romans 8:3–4*)

What does Paul say? He says that the law was powerless because it needed willing hearts. And men do not naturally have willing hearts. They have a sinful nature ('flesh '–KJV). But that did not defeat God. Far from it!

God sent His Son as a sin offering, so that He might righteously give us hearts inclined to serve Him. A believer has a heart inclined to righteousness. A believer's walk is different. He does not 'live according to the sinful nature but according to the Spirit.' In other words, God has not left the believer to himself. If you are a Christian, the Lord has remade you, so that you habitually live a life that aims to glorify Him. Now compare that grand fact with your own native weakness. And ascribe the difference to the greatness of God!

It is necessary, of course, to teach men the greatness of God by His works outside themselves. *God is glorious in all that He does.* We must never lose sight of that! Certainly 'the heavens declare the glory of God' and 'the skies proclaim the work of his hands' (*Psalm 19:1*). But men will not see God's greatness there. The heavens are everywhere shouting the majesty and power of their Creator, but men are blind. They do not see it. They suppress the truth.

Who is it that admires the greatness of God in the heavens? The soul who is converted; the simple man whom God has made wise. You are such a man if you have committed yourself to Jesus Christ. Right now, if you are a Christian, God is at work in you, teaching you to live according to the Spirit. In the light of Scripture I dare not say less. Every believer, each in his own degree, is the handiwork of God. It is true that God has not yet finished His work in you. There is still much to be done. But one measure of the greatness of the Lord is the powerful change He has already wrought in you. And the greatness of God is what the Bible is all about.

12: *Are all Christians Alike?*

If God is at work in each of His people – and He is – are all Christians alike? Are there no differences in them? There certainly seem to be. Two men converted to Christ on the same day seem to progress at different rates. Does it merely *seem* that way, or is it a fact? We need to look at these questions. In fact, we are forced to look at them. But in doing so we shall learn more of the character of the God we serve.

The proverb says, 'Variety is the spice of life.' Did you ever notice that God is the Author of variety? Consider the plant kingdom. Plants show great variety. Take their sizes, for instance. Some flowers are too tiny to be seen with the naked eye. You must use a microscope to see their beauty. Other flowers are thousands of times larger – and still beautiful.

Plants vary in shape as well. Some are thin; others are thick or bushy. Some run along the ground; others tower majestically in the air.

Plants also differ in function. Some provide food. Some provide shelter. Some provide fibres from which men make clothing. The plant kingdom shows enormous variety. The source of this variety is God. He made it. He superintends it. He uses it to serve His own purposes.

God is a God of variety in the church as well. Men in Christ differ; no two are alike. No two, I think, will ever be alike. Once, in talking with teenagers, I found one who thought that everyone in heaven would be identical. She was sure that that was what we taught. After all, doesn't the Bible say that we shall all be like the Lord Jesus? Doesn't it tell us that we shall have a body like His? This girl had reasoned that we would be so much alike that we would not know our loved ones and friends. We would all *look* alike. Could this be true?

What does the Bible mean when it says, 'We shall be like him' (*1 John 3:2*)? It means two things. First, we shall be like the Lord Jesus in our moral character. Second, it means we will have bodies with the same properties as His resurrection body.

Our great goal is to be perfectly like Christ in our moral character. God is making us like Him. The work will be completed when we enter His presence. What a day that will be! Dr Andrew Bonar's daughter illustrates this with a delightful story about her father.

> When the Queen came to Edinburgh on one occasion, he took his two youngest daughters with him to see her. As they were walking about, they met his old friend, Mr Walker of Perth, and Dr Bonar said to him, 'You see I've brought my children in to see the Queen.' 'Very good!' was Mr Walker's reply. 'Yes,' said Dr Bonar, 'we saw her, but we were not changed; but "when we see *Him* we shall be *like* Him."'[1]

What a great day is coming! *Made like Him!*

Then, too, our new bodies will not be subject to death. In this present life all of us are dying. Perhaps you have already lost a limb or an eye. Some among us even have plastic parts! But all that will change. Then the Lord Jesus 'will transform our lowly bodies so that they will be like his glorious body' (*Philippians 3:21*). No more pain or exhaustion then!

[1] The story is from p. 478 in *Andrew A. Bonar, Diary and Life*, edited by Marjory Bonar and published by the Banner of Truth Trust.

We bring God-given differences with us when we come to Christ. Of course, we bring much else also. All that is sinful will be destroyed. But there is much that is not sinful in our differences. We differ in temperament and in personality. We differ in talent. Some of this we were born with; it was the gift of God. Have you ever said to a friend, 'When God made you He threw away the mould'? Perhaps you said that as a joke. But taken simply as an observation, it is true. God had as many different 'moulds' as He had men.

Here again we meet the greatness of God. Suppose I were to build something, a sailing-boat, for instance. Well, I might make a good one. And years later, perhaps, I could sketch the design of another. A genius at sailboat design might work out a hundred or more useful plans in a lifetime. He would be applauded by his industry for outstanding work. Rightly so!

God, however, has made billions of men, every one different from all others. If He wanted to, He could fashion billions more, each one unique. In fact, if Christ does not return soon, it seems likely that He will do so. We may well call our Creator 'the God of variety!' Not only do men differ when they come to Christ, God makes them to differ after they are converted. Remember how Paul compares the church to a human body. Here are his words:

> The body is a unit, though it is made up of many parts; and though all its parts are many, they form one body. So it is with Christ. (*1 Corinthians 12:12*)

The hand, the foot, the eye and the ear are all parts of one body. Each has its own place; every part is needed.

In the same way, the church has diverse members. Each has his own gift, every one his own place. Each is the work of God. 'There are different kinds of gifts, but the same

Spirit' (*1 Corinthians 12:4*). The Holy Spirit makes each member of the body of Christ to function differently. He has given each Christian some gift or gifts to build up the church. No believer is excluded:

> All these [gifts] are the work of one and the same Spirit, and he gives them to each man, just as he determines. (*1 Corinthians 12:11*)

The Holy Spirit works in differing ways through each of God's people. And He does it as He pleases. A man may desire additional gifts and additional usefulness. It is in the hands of the Spirit whether He will receive them.

Are all Christians alike? Surely not! But that raises the question of pride and boasting. Since God bestows His gifts as He pleases, we have nothing to boast of. God's grace has measured them out. And Paul warns us to keep that fact clearly in mind:

> Do not think of yourself more highly than you ought, but rather think of yourself with sober judgment . . . Just as each of us has one body with many members, and these members do not all have the same function, so in Christ we who are many form one body, and each member belongs to all the others. We have different gifts, according to the grace given us. (*Romans 12:3–6*)

We see, then, that believers differ in at least two ways. We were not all born alike as humans, and we do not all have the same gifts as Christians.

Believers also differ in a third way. We differ in our progress in holy living. Some are more like Christ than others. But how can this be, if God is at work in each of us? The Lord has nowhere told us the whole answer to this question. Instead He has shown us our responsibility. We are to strive against sin. We are to put on the armour of

God. We are to keep praying. We are to fight the fight of faith. We are to give up ourselves, body and soul, to Him.

Do these good things that we are to do fully explain why Christians differ? No, they do not. We are plainly taught that if we succeed at these things – and we shall succeed in varying degrees, as I have shown – the glory is to go to God. But to the extent that we fail – and we shall fail to some degree – the fault will be ours. We know our responsibilities. We must strive to fulfil them. We are not to blame the Lord when we fail.

But when we succeed we must praise God. The Christian life is a co-operative effort between the Christian and God. This much is clear, however: God is the predominating factor. If that were not so there could be no certainty of our success. We could never be sure of being characteristically righteous. God's work, then, is the chief factor in the differences among believers. Paul put it this way:

> For who makes you different from anyone else? What do you have that you did not receive? And if you did receive it, why do you boast as though you did not? (*1 Corinthians 4:7*)

When Paul asks these questions he shows us that God makes Christians to differ. Yet can anyone doubt that Paul held men responsible? Paul was not a mere spectator, watching God at work. Nor would he let us sit by, on the sidelines. Instead he sets the highest of high goals in front of us: 'Whatever you do, do it all for the glory of God' (*1 Corinthians 10:31*).

In nature we see that growth does not go on at a steady pace. I saw that in my children. I might have asked myself, 'What size shoe will Joy wear nine months from now?' But there was no way to tell. She grew at a rate different from either Christina or Mark. God gave my boy and my girls the gifts of life and growth. But the growth developed in fits and starts. My rising clothing and food bills proved that they *did* develop!

God's people have the gifts of spiritual life and growth. These gifts are much like their physical counterparts. Both are co-operative efforts. We feed our bodies; we feed our souls. We try to shelter our bodies from harm; we try to shelter our souls from sin. In both cases the gifts of life and growth are highly important. And in both cases, God is the predominating factor.

Of course there are differences between physical and spiritual growth. God prevails in the Christian life in a way that does not apply to physical existence. I may neglect my physical life and die. But God will not let that happen to the believer. 'For it is God who works in you to will and to act according to his good purpose' (*Philippians 2:13*). God keeps up His activity in the Christian, so that the Christian will go on living and growing.

But the Christian grows irregularly. He too grows in fits and starts. His growth may be marred by setbacks. You can imagine Bill's Christian life as a line going upward at a 45-degree angle. That looks steady and straight. But put a magnifying glass to any portion of the line. Now what do you see? Magnified, the line is jagged. A rise, then a setback, then another rise and setback – that is how it goes on.

Janet's Christian growth might be shown by a line rising at a 50-degree angle. A third Christian's life might best be compared to a line moving upward at 40 degrees. In each case a close-up would reveal the rises and setbacks. But the overall pattern is upward, or it is not the Christian life. This is true because God is at work in His people.

There *are* differences in Christians. They may be significant. But compared to the old life, and compared with the life of the unsaved man, they are *relatively* small.

The Lord Jesus showed this in one of His stories, the parable of the sower. He spoke of a farmer who went to his field to sow seed. Some of the seed fell in the roadway, some on shallow soil, some among weeds and some on good ground. The seed on the roadway, on the shallow soil, and among the weeds bore no ripe fruit. But the seed on the good ground sprang up into healthy plants. Yet even among these seeds there was a difference in productivity. Of this seed Jesus said, 'It produced a crop – a hundred, sixty or thirty times what was sown' (*Matthew 13:8*).

As the farmer prepares his good ground for the seed, so Christ prepares the hearts of His people for His word. Let Him tell you the result:

> But what was sown on the good soil is the man who hears the word and understands it. He produces a crop, yielding a hundred, sixty or thirty times what was sown. (*Matthew 13:23*)

We see two things in these words of Jesus. First, all the seed on good soil was fruitful. Every man who receives and understands the gospel is a fruitful Christian. There are no exceptions. Of course, if he does not understand the gospel he is not a Christian at all. The seed that fell among thorns represents men who do not understand what they hear. They are false professors who eventually turn back to their real gods. True believers are fruitful believers.

Second, the fruitfulness varied with each seed. No two Christians are alike in their fruitbearing. We strive to show forth the graces called 'the fruit of the Spirit,' but we are not all equally successful. Nevertheless, Jesus teaches us that all these levels of fruitfulness are significant. A thirtyfold return is a substantial return. When God works in His people He does a mighty work. 'If a man remains in me,' Jesus said, 'and I in him, he will bear much fruit'

(*John 15:5*). That is why He came. 'I have come that [my sheep] may have life, and have it to the full' (*John 10:10*).

In a coming day Christians will vary in another way. They will differ in their rewards. Christ will reward His people with varying duties and responsibilities when He returns. Will these differences be significant? Yes and no! In themselves, yes; one reward will be quite different from another. But compared with the fate of the lost – compared with the hell that would have been ours, if Christ had not redeemed us – they will be relatively small. Our common experience of salvation will tower over all the differences left between us!

The rewards themselves will be acts of grace. Some will exceed others only by the goodness of God. Here too *God*'s will remains the predominating factor. Do you remember what the mother of James and John asked the Lord to grant her? She wanted her sons to be number two and number three in Christ's kingdom. But the Lord answered her:

> To sit at my right or left is not for me to grant. These places belong to those for whom they have been prepared by my Father. (*Matthew 20:23*)

Why did He answer in that way? He could have told James and John to strive to reach their goal. There would have been nothing wrong with that. He has promised high places, for instance, to those who are genuinely servants to all believers. But instead Jesus emphasised the Father's grace in giving His rewards. God will reward all believers. But of all the rewards Jesus will say, 'These places belong to those for whom they have been prepared by my Father.'

13: *Who is doing the Work of God?*

The question at the head of this chapter may be answered in two ways. We may answer, 'God is doing His own work!' That answer is true and it needs to be stressed. The expression 'He has no hands but our hands,' has been badly overworked. God is perfectly competent to do anything He desires. God is God! He uses 'our hands' or bypasses them, as it pleases Him.

What I am asking is this: granted that God is doing some of His work through men and women, who are the people He is using? Are they preachers? Are they missionaries? Are they social workers or doctors or nurses? Who are they? Can they be identified? Do they smile in a certain way? Could we identify them by the looks on their faces?

One common answer is this. God is using the men and women who are doing the really important things. But that raises another question: what are the really important things? Here are five things. Rearrange them in the order of their importance:

1. Mopping a dirty floor.
2. Wiping runny noses.
3. Winning a soul to Christ.
4. Giving your employer an honest day's work.
5. Praying for a missionary.

Now that you have rearranged them, you could compare your list to mine. But I do not have a list. Let me tell you why.

It is clear, I think, that some of the activities above have a more lasting impact than others of them. In that sense, they are more important. Near the head of the list we would put 'winning a soul to Christ.' Perhaps 'wiping a runny nose' belongs at the bottom of the list. And it is well to know that, in order to give my life long-range direction. But I must also look at this another way. I must ask, 'What is the most important thing for *me* to do *now*?' I have put in italics two variables here. One has to do with *me*, my talents and abilities. Surely the Lord wants me to do what *I* can do. And just as surely, He wants me to do what I can do *now*. Perhaps at a later time I will have more skills, more opportunities. But this is the moment that I have now. I must use it or lose it for ever. If, at the moment, there is a runny nose to be wiped, it is important that I do it. And I am told to do it for the glory of God.

To do something for the glory of God is, in large part, to aim to please Him. There is nothing that God *must* have done for Himself. But there is nothing about which He is indifferent. In everything He looks to see if we are seeking to please Him. *So the man who is aiming to please God is doing the one most important thing a creature can do.* And he is doing it whether men happen to see its importance or not.

It makes a great deal of difference *to a man* whether I mop his dirty floor or point him to Christ. One is far more important to the man than the other, because he benefits from them in different ways. If I mop his floor it will get dirty again. A year from now he will have forgotten who mopped his floor. He will not remember whether it was mopped at all.

If I point him to Christ he will remember that, and be grateful for it a million years from now. Why? Because his needs differ in importance. One thing I do may serve the need of a moment; another thing I do may serve the needs of eternity.

On the other hand, *God* has no needs. He is self-sufficient. But God has given us the privilege of seeking to please Him. A successful man is a man who aims to please God. A failure is a man who does not aim to please God. A man is doing the work of God when he seeks to please his Maker. He is not doing God's work when he fails to aim at pleasing God. Suppose your four-year-old says, 'Daddy, can I do something for you?' You would be hard pressed to find some *need* that he could fill. Perhaps you would say, 'Bring me this,' or 'Hand me that.' What he brought would not be the really important thing. What would be important? The fact that he wanted to please you would be the important thing.

That is the way it is with God. What we do is not the most important thing. It may be praying for a missionary or giving our employers an honest day's work. (The act is secondary, unless it is something God has forbidden). Aiming to please Him is the thing of chief importance. Let me show you what I mean, right from the Scripture.

The story of Mary of Bethany is told in Mark chapter 14. Mary was the woman who poured a costly pound of ointment on the head and feet of the Lord Jesus. The disciples, led by Judas, complained, 'Why this waste of perfume? It could have been sold for more than a year's wages and the money given to the poor' (*Mark 14:4-5*). It would be hard to fault their logic. Think what a year's wages might do for some poor man!

But Jesus saw it differently. He glimpsed in Mary a desire to please Him. To Him her desire was so important that He would never allow it to be forgotten. Think of what He said about her:

> I tell you the truth, wherever the gospel is preached throughout the world, what she has done will also be told, in memory of her. (*Mark 14:9*)

Can you think of a more unlikely prophecy? But we are fulfilling it right now by retelling her story. It is being fulfilled every day. All because one woman wanted to please the Lord Jesus!

What Mary did was impractical. Jesus said, 'She poured perfume on my body beforehand to prepare for my burial' (*Mark 14:8*). Though the Lord was certain to die, 'beforehand' is the worst possible time to prepare a corpse! But never mind! She aimed to please Him; that was the important thing.

The Lord said through Paul, 'Whether you eat or drink or whatever you do, do it all for the glory of God' (*1 Corinthians 10:31*). In plain terms, what does that mean? It means to do what I do, to please Him. I may do any number of things, but I glorify Him when *I aim to please Him*.

Who, then, is doing the work of God? Each Christian is doing God's work, when he aims to glorify God where he is. Here is a mother wiping runny noses. Is she doing the work of God? Yes, just as truly as the preacher who preaches to thousands. In fact, we can go a step further. If she is set on pleasing the Lord, and the preacher is not, then she will be doing the work of God while he is falling under God's judgment!

We need to be crystal-clear about this. God *needs* neither preachers nor mothers. What He produces are men and women who seek to please Him. Then He chooses the circumstances into which He will put such men and women. One may be in a large place where thousands see him. Another may be hidden in a corner, unknown to the world. That does not matter. One thing is needful in both cases: the ambition to please and glorify God.

I fear that we have been brainwashed by modern advertising. The emphasis on bigness and prominence has misled the church. Mass communication has deceived us. We see men who are known by millions, and we say, 'These are the men God is using!' If God has men and women in prominent places let us thank God. But prominence is nothing, and the size of the work is nothing, when compared to this question, 'Is my eye fixed on glorifying God?'

Christian, take heart! Your circumstances are no accident. They are fitted to your need; they are shaped for your good. Now is the time and this is the place where you are called to serve the Lord. Your circumstances are God's present will for you. By all means, pray about them. Tell the Lord, if you would like to have them changed. But tell Him as well, 'Not my will, Lord, but yours!' Make up your mind, by God's grace always to give 'thanks to God the Father for everything' (*Ephesians 5:20*). In doing these things you will be doing the work of God.

Think with me about the Old Testament story of Naaman. You will find it in 2 Kings 5. Naaman was a great man. In twentieth-century America we would call him 'a five-star general.' But Naaman was a leper. 'The basest slave of Syria would not change skins with him,' said Bishop Joseph Hall, 'if he might have his honour to boot.' Leprosy offset all his other advantages. The story does not end there, however. Naaman was to be delivered from his leprosy of body and of heart.

Two people of no consequence whatever, in the eyes of men, played key roles in Naaman's deliverance. And neither of them dreamed that they were bringing a man to God. How obscure were these people? The writer of Scripture has not even given us their names!

The first was a slave girl who served in Naaman's house. One day she made a 'chance' remark: 'If only my master would see the prophet who is in Samaria! He would cure him of his leprosy' (*2 Kings 5:3*). And with that, she drops out of sight.

C.T.H.—8

In God's providence that remark was used to get Naaman to Elisha the prophet. But Namaan did not receive an immediate healing. Instead Elisha said, 'Go, wash yourself seven times in the Jordan, and your flesh will be restored and you will be cleansed' (*2 Kings 5:11*). But that did not set well with the great general. He made a mental comparison of the muddy Jordan with the clear rivers of Damascus. His conclusion? He turned back toward home in a rage.

That could have been the end of the story. But it is not. Here comes another obscure servant on the scene. Listen to him talk to Naaman:

> My father, if the prophet had told you to do some great thing, would you not have done it? How much more then, when he tells you, 'Wash and be cleansed'? (*2 Kings 5:13*)

Who was this man? A servant, a spokesmen for all Naaman's servants. What was his name? I don't know. But Naaman took his advice. He washed and was saved, not only from leprosy, but from sin. Here is his testimony: 'Now I know that there is no God in all the world except in Israel' (*2 Kings 5:15*).

Picture yourself in the place of one of those unnamed servants. You push your mop. Or you push your pencil. No one knows you. Your name will never be in lights. Is that any obstacle to God's using you? None at all! The slave girl, if she was a servant of God, had been doing God's work all along. When she mentioned the prospect of healing she was not conscious of doing something radically different from the things she normally did. In the course of doing her job, aiming to please the Lord, she took an interest in the health of another. That was not unusual. But her 'chance' remark has been left for generations to read; it was work for God.

You must not think that the Lord must work harder to use people in little known places. You must not say, 'Well, yes, I guess God could figure out a way to use even me where I am.' 'Aim at My glory,' the Lord says, 'and I *am* using you. Aim to please Me, and you are *My* minister, right where you are, in whatever you are doing!'

God memorialises common work done for His glory. We see this in the case of a woman named Dorcas. Here is her story:

> In Joppa there was a disciple named Tabitha (which, when translated, is Dorcas), who was always doing good and helping the poor. About that time she became sick and died, and her body was washed and placed in an upstairs room. Lydda was near Joppa; so when the disciples heard that Peter was in Lydda, they sent two men to him and urged him, 'Please come at once!' (*Acts 9:36–38*)

When Peter arrived he found mourners weeping 'and showing him the robes and other clothing that Dorcas had made' (*Acts 9:39*).

In twentieth-century America we can hardly imagine Dorcas' situation. A widow, and left to her needle to eke out a living! Thank God she is in heaven and away from the cares of this life! But wait, God has other plans. He wants to fix Dorcas and her obscure service indelibly in our minds. So Peter prays and speaks her name. Then 'she opened her eyes, and seeing Peter she sat up' (*Acts 9:40*). And Luke adds, 'Many people believed in the Lord' (*Acts 9:42*). Think of her, a 'nobody' who was a 'somebody' in the eyes of God! Fix Dorcas in your mind, and take heart! God raised His little-known servant to bring others to Himself and to remind us that He can use us all.

What is your job for God! I do not know. But it is not at all hard to find out. Where did God put you? In an office? Aim to please Him, and your office work becomes the work of God. In the home? Seek to glorify Him and your housework is 'His work' too. In the factory? Work 'for the Lord, not for men, since you know you will receive an inheritance from the Lord as a reward. *It is the Lord Christ you are serving*' (*Colossians 3:23–24*).

I do not mean to discourage you from what is commonly called 'Christian work.' Far from it! By all means, witness. Distribute your tracts and teach your Sunday school classes. Do anything that may be used to point men to Christ. But when you do those things, keep this in mind: your day-by-day chore is also 'Christian work.' 'Whatever you do, whether in word or deed,' says Paul, 'do it all in the name of the Lord Jesus' (*Colossians 3:17*). In doing that, you will be doing the work of God. Christian, take heart!

14: Once Saved, Always Saved?

Can a saved man ever be lost? Will the God of the Bible start a work within a man that He does not intend to finish? Can a man be saved, live for himself, and still go to be with the Lord? Is 'once saved, always saved' true? These questions and others like them have often disturbed Christians. What is the truth?

Let me give you a brief answer first. When God saves a man, that man is saved for ever. God does not start the work of salvation in a man only to abandon it later. Strictly speaking, then, 'once saved, always saved' is true.

But there is another side to this truth, a side that is often overlooked and is sometimes vigorously opposed. God saves from both sin and hell. If God does not separate men from their sin, He does not take them to heaven. And the process of separating a believer from his sin goes ahead in this life. It is not postponed until death. Right now, 'if anyone is in Christ, he is a new creation' (*2 Corinthians 5:17*). God 'created us in Christ Jesus to do good works' (*Ephesians 2:10*), good works to be done while we live in the flesh.

In these pages I am setting before you this fact: a saved man is a changed man. I am warning you of the consequences of forgetting it. But now let me tell you why I believe that no saved man will ever be lost. This is one of God's great promises. You need to understand it and receive its comfort.

The picture of the human heart that God gives us in His word is not at all encouraging. Natural men are said to be dead, utterly unresponsive to God. When God comes to save us He finds us 'dead in transgressions' (*Ephesians 2:5*). Because we are dead toward God, we wander away from Him – inevitably. We are like sheep. 'We all, like sheep, have gone astray, each of us has turned to his own way' (*Isaiah 53:6*). The sheep has no instinctive means for finding the shepherd. It has power to carry itself away, but no ability to come home again. A lost sheep is like a ship without compass or stars. A ship like that will never reach home port.

The Bible compares the Lord Jesus to a shepherd in search of his lost sheep. The shepherd will leave ninety-nine sheep in the sheepfold to search for one of his own that is missing.

Jesus spoke of Himself as a shepherd to His people. Here are His words:

> My sheep listen to my voice; I know them, and they follow me. I give them eternal life, and they shall never perish; no one can snatch them out of my Father's hand. (*John 10:27–28*)

These verses speak of Jesus' relation to the sheep after He has brought them to His fold. Let us see what they say.

First, we learn something about the attitude of the sheep. They *hear* and they *follow*. These are two great facts. Before God draws men to Christ they are deaf to the Lord's voice. With that deafness in mind Jesus often said, 'He who has ears, let him hear!' Men choose not to hear the voice of Christ until they are born again. But Jesus' sheep hear His voice. Why? Because God has given them new hearts. As a result of 'hearing' they follow Christ. If you are saved, you follow the Lord. Wandering sheep are unconverted sheep; saved sheep do the will of their shepherd, they follow Him. This, of course, is the work of God in their lives. No man can produce this change. Only God can do it.

Second, we learn the attitude of the Lord Jesus toward His sheep. 'I know them,' He says, and 'I give them eternal life.' Here are two more important facts. The word 'know' in Scripture often denotes a special closeness between the one who knows and the one who is known. As an example, let us take Psalm 1:6. 'The Lord knoweth the way of the righteous' (KJV). Doesn't God know everyone's way? Yes, but He is intimately associated with the life of the righteous man. There is a special closeness between the righteous man and the Lord.

Because Jesus 'knows' His sheep, He gives them eternal life. We must not think of eternal life simply as long life. All men shall live for ever; that is, they shall exist for ever. That is true of both saved and unsaved. When Jesus says, 'I give them eternal life' He has much more than mere existence in view. He means that He gives His followers a special quality of life, the quality of life that fits a man for eternal fellowship with God.

What follows from Jesus' gift of eternal life? His sheep 'shall never perish.' To put it another way, 'No one can snatch them out of my Father's hand.' Words could not be plainer: Jesus' sheep are safe for ever. He will not cast them away, and no one will be able to tear them from His and His Father's hands.

Many texts in the Bible teach this truth. Let me suggest a few more. Here is James 1:2. 'Consider it pure joy, my brothers, whenever you face trials of many kinds.' Think about that. How can we be happy when we are tried? We could be nothing but fearful if the trial might undo us. What 'joy' could we have if the trial might be the means of taking us from Christ into eternal hell? The reason for 'pure joy' in trial is this: in God's people trial 'develops perseverance' (*James 1:3*). It does not lead to destruction. (A similar thought is found in 1 Peter 1:6–7; 4:12–13.)

Romans 8:28 is a familiar verse. 'We know that in all things God works for the good of those who love him, who have been called according to his purpose.' That is a precious promise. Do you see what it implies? It tells us that nothing will happen to us that will lead us to hell. God works everything for our good. What if someone says, 'The promise is to those who continue to love God'; will that make any difference? No, it will not! If God works everything for our good, then nothing will lead us to give up our love for God. Even if you make continuing love for God a condition, this verse shows that God will keep us loving Him, else something would lead to our eternal loss. Romans 8:28 shows us that nothing will work against us in the long run.

And what about 1 John 3:6, the verse that we looked at earlier? 'No one who lives in him keeps on sinning. No one who continues to sin has either seen him or known him.' John gives us a glimpse of men as God sees them. There are two classes here, no more. There are those who do not keep on sinning, and there are those who do keep on sinning. The first class 'lives in him.' The second class has never 'seen him or known him.' There are none who live in Christ and habitually sin. There are none who habitually sin who once knew Him. In other words, there are none who once knew Christ, and now no longer know Him.[1]

The other side of the truth that God keeps His people safe for ever is also important: no man is to offer the habitual sinner assurance. God's word is clear. A man who belongs to Christ will live for Christ. 'The mind of sinful

---

[1]The Appendix, p 154ff, is a detailed study of 1 John 3:6 in the light of previous scholarly discussion of it. The general reader may wish to skip this more technical material.

man is death, but the mind controlled by the Spirit is life and peace' (*Romans 8:6*). If a man loves God he hates sin; if a man loves sin he hates God.

At one time I did not understand this. I would tell a man who apparently had no intention of living for God: 'Bill, you know you are a Christian. You made a decision for Christ years ago.' By speaking in that way I encouraged men to be unconcerned about their eternal destiny. I pleaded with them about sin. I wished to see them live holy lives. But my words of assurance undid the good I hoped to do. I did not realise that salvation meant salvation from sin as well as salvation from hell.

The biblical view differs from the view I once held. No one has the right to tell an unrepentant sinner that God will take him to heaven. No one has the right to imply it. It makes no difference who the man may be, or how faithfully he has attended the services of the church. No one may tell him he is saved. Instead we must say, 'If you live according to the sinful nature, you will die' (*Romans 8:13*).

The Bible is clear on this. Why did I think otherwise? Why did I seek to reassure unrepentant men? Why did I pervert a teaching that was meant for godly people? I want to answer these questions and sound an alarm to help you in living and teaching.

Earlier I showed you that the writers of Scripture often give men the titles they claim for themselves. If men call themselves 'brothers' or 'disciples' or 'saints', Scripture addresses them by those names. But the Bible does more. It warns 'brothers' and 'disciples' and 'saints' that their professions of faith may mean nothing. The lives of real 'saints' bear out their profession. If I am a genuine 'disciple' I will prove it by aiming to please Christ. If you are a true 'brother' you will keep on serving God. If we are false we will someday fall by the wayside.

Until about 150 years ago most Christians understood this. Preachers addressed their church members as professing Christians. They warned them that their profession might prove to be false. All evangelical churches warned believers about the consequences of sin. Methodist churches, that held that a genuine believer could fall away and be lost gave such warning. So did Presbyterian and Baptist churches, though they believed in eternal security. These churches disagreed on many things. But they were united on this: 'If you live according to the sinful nature, you will die'.

Then something happened. Near the beginning of the Nineteenth Century a subtle change began. Up to that time men were told to 'repent and believe the gospel', to be saved. But each man was left to himself to 'repent and believe.' Men were told that God alone could see their faith and repentance. So men were shut up to God. They were not told to *do* anything, apart from turning to God. There were no methods for 'seeing' a soul saved. When a man professed faith in Christ he was welcomed according to his profession. But he was solemnly warned to persevere in his faith, to go on in godliness. In other words, he was dealt with just as Scripture deals with professing Christians.

Gradually that changed. Christian workers began to feel that the preaching of the gospel was not enough. Something else had to be added so that men could be immediately assured that they had been born again. They were still told to repent and believe, but they were not left there. They were given something to do, something that would clinch the matter.

Before long many preachers became proficient in the new methods. Converts multiplied. By leading men to say 'the sinner's prayer,' by urging them to 'make a public stand,' by giving men a verse to cling to, suddenly there were 'Christians' everywhere. Churches, attended by few, began to fill. A new day had apparently dawned. Not all Christian workers used these methods. But they were hard to resist because of their large 'results'.

Preachers still preached 'repent and believe.' But, in practice, they led souls to Christ in another way. First, repentance was changed to 'acknowledge that you're a sinner.' The Bible teaches that an unregenerate man will not truly repent (turn from his sin) without the work of the Spirit. But many reprobates will acknowledge that they are sinners – proudly or ignorantly! Christian workers, however, were now taught to accept an admission of guilt as sufficient proof of an enquirer's commitment to Christ. In this way, in many quarters, numbers who gave no evidence of possessing changed hearts, were told to regard themselves as young Christians.

Again, in personal counselling, faith was often dropped. If a 'convert' had difficulty in understanding what it was to believe, he was immediately given something to do. 'Never mind,' he was told in effect. 'Pray this prayer, and if you are sincere Christ will save you right now.' Of course, any sinner who believed in hell was sincere in wanting deliverance from it. And so, without repentance, and with the barest kind of faith possible, millions became 'Christians'.

This produced a problem. Soon Bible-believing churches had two kinds of Christians. There had always been hypocrites in the churches, but now the great mass of 'Christians' in many places were really unchanged. This posed a theological problem. How could men and women be Christians and be unchanged? One possible solution was devised: these were 'carnal Christians.' Such men were eternally secure, but they were taking the carnal way to heaven. 'Spiritual Christians' formed a minority in evangelical churches. 'Carnal Christians' had taken over!

And that situation remains today. Ask many a preacher, 'Aren't most Christians carnal?' Without batting an eye, he will answer with a resounding 'Yes!'

Earlier Christians spoke of the 'perseverance of the saints.' They meant that if any man's profession of faith in Christ was real, that man would go on living a godly life. That is the teaching of Scripture. Now, that had to be changed. In its place we heard of the 'eternal security of the believer.' Even that was soon shaved down to 'eternal security.' Nothing was said about the man persevering in either holiness or faith. So today we hear 'once saved, always saved.'

What is the effect of this? First, men are encouraged to believe that they are saved without repentance. They are given a verse of Scripture and told that as long as that verse is in the Bible they are safe. God help those of us who have misled them! Some few will be saved, thank God, because they did repent and believe. More will suppose that they are Christians only to wake up in hell. Still others will imagine that they have tried Christianity because they have been put through such a scheme. They will say, 'I gave it a chance, and there's nothing to it!'

There will be a further effect. Since we have given men assurance, we will certainly not try to take it away from them. We will hesitate to preach to our people as men and women who may be lost. We will teach them to rest on a 'first-time decision.' We will act as if the Bible did not say, 'Examine yourselves to see whether you are in the faith' (*2 Corinthians 13:5*). We will forget the words of Peter, 'Therefore, my brothers, be all the more eager to make your calling and election sure' (*2 Peter 1:10*).

Does this sound harsh? I wish it did not. I do not want to shake the faith of any child of God. I have no desire to supply names (except my own) or to hurt any preacher of the gospel. But our present preaching of 'eternal security' must be abandoned. We must warn men that no matter how many 'altars' they have knelt at, how many decision cards they have signed, or how faithfully they have attended the preaching of the Word, if they have not repented and put their faith squarely on Christ, they have not been saved.

I do not fear for the assurance of real believers. Assurance, given by God, is not a fragile thing. Paul says to all God's people, 'The Spirit himself testifies with our spirit that we are God's children' (*Romans 8:16*). The Spirit of God will not forsake us, leaving us to our own resources. On the other hand, with the Lord's help we must seek to bring hypocrites to a condition of healthy doubt.

I wish I could personally speak to every preacher of the gospel. I would say, 'Friend, beware. It is not just the destiny of the visitors to your church that is in your hands. It is the destiny of each of your hearers. Preach Christ to all of them. Command them to repent. Tell them what you are doing. Make them understand. In no other way can you be free from the blood of all men.'

15: *How the Chickens Have Come Home*

The old saying is, 'The chickens come home to roost.' It means, of course, that when you send an idea out into the world it may return to haunt you. It may carry with it consequences that you did not dream of. One day, unlooked for, the idea will come back to upset you. It will return just like the chickens come home to the henhouse at night.

We have sent a false notion out into the Christian world. We have said that there are two classes of Christians, the spiritual and the carnal. We have implied that the average Christian is on the lower level, the carnal level. And we have sought ways to lift him to the higher plateau. We have had our 'victorious life conferences' and our meetings to teach men and women to be Spirit-baptised or Spirit-filled. And after all these gatherings we have still said, 'The typical Christian is carnal.' By our teaching we have created a vacuum of longing in the lives of many of our people. And we have left it unfilled.

A new movement has appeared to fill that vacuum, neo-pentecostalism, or the Charismatic Movement. In recent years this modern tongues and healing movement has spread throughout the world with its distinctive message. Because I see in it so much of the seed that we have carelessly planted, I want to devote this chapter to discussing it. In the process, I think, we shall see how some of us have paved its way.

First, let me define the Charismatic Movement as well as I can, so that there will be no doubt as to what I am talking about. There is some difficulty here. The movement is not organised; it has no published creed. But I think you will recognise it from my description.

The Charismatic Movement is that movement that professes to restore to worldwide Christianity the baptism or filling of the Holy Spirit accompanied by supernatural signs, especially the sign of 'speaking in tongues.' Charismatic Christians do not deny the reality of Christian experience in other Christians. Instead, they hold that the New Testament teaches a Christianity that goes far beyond the Christianity most Christians know. Charismatic Christians fear that much of the Christianity around them represents a cold, intellectual knowledge of the gift of the Spirit as He was given at Pentecost. By their joyous testimony Charismatic Christians hope to see the Spirit and His gifts restored to all Christians in these latter days.

Unlike the older Pentecostalism, the Charismatic Movement in America has not majored on the formation of churches. There is no formal membership in the movement. There are no dues to be paid. A typical adherent may be a member in good standing of one of the old-line Protestant denominations. He may be a member of a Pentecostal church. He may be a Roman Catholic. He may be a member of no church at all. What binds the Charismatic Movement together is an experience, the experience of 'the baptism.' That experience, and a desire to share it, makes you a member of Charismatic Christianity.

The first thing that strikes me as I look at the movement is this: its theology is again the old 'two-level' doctrine in a new dress. Charismatic writers agree on this familiar theme: there are two kinds of Christians, the Spirit-baptised and the non-Spirit-baptised. They also agree that the majority of Christians fall into the second category. They see it as their mission to lift men from the lower level of Christian experience to the higher. In that way they are very much like other evangelicals. They often use the same terms to describe what has happened to them. Very often they distinguish between Christians with power and Christians without power. They make much of a life controlled by the Holy Spirit.

If we ask where the Charismatic Movement got its theology, there is a surprising answer. A number of names from the late nineteenth century keep popping up in older Pentecostal literature – A. J. Gordon, F. B. Meyer, A. B. Simpson, Andrew Murray and R. A. Torrey. These men were leading evangelicals of their day. They are repeatedly quoted in Pentecostal manuals of doctrine. And these are the same men who taught fundamentalism and evangelicalism that there are two kinds of Christians.

R. A. Torrey is remembered with affection by conservatives in America. A graduate of Yale University, Torrey was an associate of D. L. Moody both in evangelism and in the work of the Moody Bible Institute in Chicago. Torrey was also an influential writer. He published forty books. He is widely quoted by contemporary fundamentalists.

Torrey's book, *What The Bible Teaches*, has a passage that one writer, F. D. Bruner, estimates has been quoted more often by Pentecostal writers than any other statement by a non-Pentecostal. It runs as follows:

The Baptism with the Holy Spirit is an operation of the Holy Spirit distinct from and subsequent and additional to His regenerating work . . . A man may be regenerated by the Holy Spirit and still not be baptised with the Holy Spirit. In regeneration there is an impartation of life, and the one who receives it is saved; in the Baptism with the Holy Spirit there is an impartation of power and the one who receives it is fitted for service.

Every true believer has the Holy Spirit. But not every believer has the Baptism with the Holy Spirit, though every believer . . . may have.

Here Torrey has stated the doctrine of two kinds of believers as clearly as it can be stated. Doubtless he never dreamed that his words would continually be pressed into service by Pentecostalism. But it is not hard to see why they use them. Torrey's doctrine and the doctrine of the Charismatic Movement have an enormous amount in common.[1]

Charismatic writers have added to Torrey's doctrine, but they still hold what Torrey held, that there are two classes of believers, the Spirit-baptised and the non-Spirit-baptised. I had a practical illustration of this close tie between Torrey and neo-Pentecostalism the same week I wrote this paragraph. I visited a healing meeting in a nearby Presbyterian church. On a book table chiefly devoted to Charismatic writers, I saw a familiar title. It was Torrey's *The Baptism With The Holy Spirit*. First published in 1897, there it was in sparkling new garb to entice late-twentieth-century readers.

If there are two kinds of Christians, it is not surprising that men touched by God's Spirit would seek the higher level. It makes little difference how you describe those two levels. If only some Christians are Spirit-baptised, the others will seek to be Spirit-baptised. If only some have power that all may have at any time, the others will want that power. If they have to go out of traditional channels to get it, they will do so. Such teaching creates a thirst that must be quenched.

[1] I have quoted the Torrey passage from F. D. Bruner, *A Theology of the Holy Spirit*, Grand Rapids, 1970, p. 335. Bruner's book is an important contribution to the understanding of the Charismatic Movement. In chapter six of this volume I have explained the limited sense in which I recognise that not all Christians are equally 'Spirit-filled'.

The Charismatic Movement offers to quench this thirst in a way traditional Christianity cannot match. It offers a 'miracle' to prove that the higher level has been attained. That miracle is 'speaking in tongues.' What other 'deeper life movement' has anything to compare with a miracle that lets you know that you are now on the higher plane?

Some have tried to meet the claim of this movement by calling it a counterfeit of the real thing. Their reasoning has been this: since there is a 'deeper life' for Christians, naturally Satan would imitate it. The devil often does copy what God does. His copy is a perversion, but it accomplishes his work. Why couldn't that be the case here? Why couldn't the Charismatic Movement be Satan's copy of God's 'deeper' work?

One answer would be to question the charity of this approach. After all, who has authorised us to make this kind of blanket condemnation of many who also give evidence of loving and serving the Lord Jesus? But my point here is of a different kind. It is a practical one. Those who try to meet the Charismatic Movement with this idea are doomed to failure. As long as we hold and teach that there are two kinds of Christians they will always win. None of the other deeper life movements has a 'miracle' to authenticate it. Hungry men will go to the group that can prove to them by a sign from heaven that they are now on a higher level of the Christian life.

What we both must do is submit ourselves to the Word of God. We must both renounce the idea that there is something for us which was not given when Christ was given. We must no longer deny the work of God in each of His people. We must say what God says: 'Those who are led by the Spirit of God are sons of God' (*Romans 8:14*). True Christians walk with the Spirit habitually. God is directly at work in all His people. All have His power. This is the answer that must be given to the idea of two kinds of Christians in all its forms.

The truth of God will win out with true believers. We need not fear for the ark of God. It will not fall. But God does not work at a pace that suits us. He suits Himself. 'Two-level Christianity' is doomed. It is doomed because it denies the sufficiency of Christ. We may not live to see it die, but its death is sure.

Already there are voices within the Charismatic Movement seeking to quiet some of the claims that early adherents made for it. More and more Charismatic teachers are saying: 'Do not think you are especially spiritual because you have the "baptism".' Experience shows that men with a 'deeper life' are, after all, just as human as other believers. If these voices prevail, however, this movement will lose its basic appeal. That appeal is to quench the thirst for a higher-level Christianity. When the movement no longer offers that, it will lose its uniqueness and melt into the larger world of Christianity much like the 'tongues' movements before it.

But the death may be slow in coming. The very men who say, 'Do not think you are especially spiritual because you have the "baptism",' are the same men who continually imply the opposite. They speak of the great joy that comes, and only comes, with the 'baptism'. They remind us that we are commanded to 'rejoice in the Lord always' (*Philippians 4:4*). And they tell us that we must be 'baptised' to carry out that command. In other words, we are now disobedient Christians, but we can be made obedient by 'the baptism in the Spirit.'

These men remind us that we are to 'pray in the Spirit.' How may we do that? By praying in tongues, they say. They may not want to follow their reasoning to its logical conclusion, but the point is clear: 'You can't carry out these spiritual commands, you cannot be the kind of

Christian you ought to be, until you have the 'baptism".' As long as they imply things like that, they will teach their followers that they *are* especially spiritual. No disclaimer will do any good. Their disciples will believe what the leaders apparently believe, not what they occasionally say.

One Charismatic teacher asks: 'Do you want to glorify Christ? Do you want to know the mind of Christ? . . . Then let the Spirit have *His* way and let *Him* pray in you and through you in "unknown tongues".' Can any Christian be spiritual and refuse to let the 'Spirit have *His* way'? Surely a man who lets the 'Spirit have His way' is a spiritual man. No matter what these men say, they plainly imply that 'Spirit-baptised' Christians are more spiritual than 'non-baptised' believers. Much of their success depends on producing this feeling. If they ever successfully deny it, the movement will lose its hold on millions.

But what of their 'miracle'? What can we say about speaking in tongues. Doesn't that experience really prove that the Charismatic Movement is on the right track? Can others produce a miracle to authenticate their teaching? How can we answer questions like these?

Christians, it seems to me, may reasonably differ on the continuance of miraculous gifts, including tongues, after the close of the apostolic period. Charismatics are not to be condemned simply because they do not answer that question in the way that I would do. At least, that is my opinion, though others would oppose them adamantly on that score. But certain other things must be said. First, we must tell them what we must tell ourselves: no miracle, true or false, can authenticate teaching that opposes God's Word. The purpose of the Word is clear, to teach truth. Whatever disagrees with God's Word is false. Such a false teaching is the 'two-level' teaching. There are not two distinct levels of believers according to the New Testament. Miracles, however many or however breathtaking, can never prove what Scripture shows to be false.

But there is more to be said. Speaking in tongues, as it is commonly done today, is no miracle at all. I know that sounds harsh, but it is true. I leave to one side the question whether there are *any* legitimate instances of tongues-speaking in the twentieth century. But by extensive reading and personal observation I have learned one thing that an outsider might not otherwise guess. *Men are taught to speak in tongues.* Many testimonies to the experience carefully omit that fact. In reading those testimonies you might conclude that to burst out in tongues is a spontaneous thing. But it is not so! In the overwhelming majority of cases men and women make those strange sounds after careful instruction. That instruction does not centre on the Holy Spirit or God. That instruction has nothing to do with the spiritual life. Instead, it has to do with the mouth, the vocal chords and the use of the lungs.

Let me cite instructions that are commonly used. First, the prospect will be told that *he* must do the speaking. No, you did not misread that. That is very important. In fact, the Charismatic Movement often derides the earlier Pentecostals for teaching otherwise. The Pentecostals frequently 'tarried' as if they expected the Holy Spirit to speak through them. 'Not so,' says the Charismatic teacher. 'Don't wait for the Spirit to speak. Speak yourself!'

But how can one speak in an unknown language? By following directions. Typically the directions are these:

1. Open your mouth wide. Most gifts are received by hand. This one is received with the mouth!
2. Take a deep breath – as deep as possible. Keep taking deep breaths until you feel the presence of God.

3. Tell God in your spirit: 'I am receiving the Holy Spirit right now by faith.' [Some teachers omit this step.]
4. Now show that you believe the Lord has baptised you in the Spirit by beginning to speak. Only do not speak English!

What is the result of this kind of instruction? If the directions are carefully followed, the person 'speaks in tongues'. What does he do when he speaks in tongues? He produces syllables of his own making. If he keeps it up, he becomes proficient at it. At that point there is someone on hand to assure him that the miracle has happened, just as in the Book of Acts!

I know that the above description sounds grossly carnal. There is nothing that compares with it in Acts. Do not think that I am making fun of something that is sacred to others when I describe it in such fleshly terms. The instructions I have just given are all taken from teachers within the movement. They would not agree that the speaker made up his own syllables, though to an outsider that seems obvious. But so far as the instructions are concerned, they might be glad that I have included them in this book.

I have already said: 'The chickens have come home to roost.' In doing so, I have said to myself and others, 'We are, at least in part, the authors of the Charismatic Movement. We taught them, too well, that there are two kinds of Christians. Do we dare complain if they have believed us?'

But this book is not primarily an attack on the Charismatic Movement. That movement is only one form that this false teaching has taken. And I, with others, am to blame.

We must stop degrading Christ, for that is what we do when we seek a qualitatively different level of Christianity above our fellow Christians. We do not mean to degrade Him. We do not mean to set Him aside. But we are guilty of these offences. May the Lord help us to rediscover the truth: those who have Christ have all things! Paul the apostle wrote:

> All things are yours, whether Paul or Apollos or Cephas or the world or life or death or the present or the future – all are yours, and you are of Christ, and Christ is of God. (*1 Corinthians 3:22–23*)

The 'all things' may be given to us over a lifetime, but that does not change the fact. All God has is ours. There are no more conditions for unique experiences.

> He who began a good work in you will carry it on to completion until the day of Christ Jesus. (*Philippians 1:6*)

Christian: take heart!

16: 'Make your Calling and Election Sure'

'Christian, take heart!' I have said that all through this book. The truth that God is at work in each of His people should make us take heart. It is one of God's grand encouragements. Think of it! – the Almighty Lord at work in former rebels to make them like Himself. Unthinkable, yet true!

This truth, however, is only of use to you if you are a Christian. Otherwise it means nothing. God's promises are for God's people. The good things of God, if you miss them, will only make eternity more bitter. There is no more fearful prospect than to see and to know what good things the Lord gives His people, and through unbelief to fail to receive them.

The authors of Scripture wrote with this fact in mind. They spoke to men as 'brothers', as 'saints' and as 'elect'. They spoke to men according to their profession. They gave professed believers the names those professors claimed for themselves. But they did more. These inspired writers did not drop their pens until they had warned all 'brothers', all 'saints' and all the 'elect' that they must go on with Christ. That was the only way to prove that any professed believer was a 'brother' indeed. Paul and Peter and James and John did not want the blood of any man on their hands. Better that they be mocked or ignored while preaching Christ, than that they preach salvation to any man on any terms but God's terms.

What are God's terms of salvation? Throughout the

Scriptures two words recur: 'repent' and 'believe'. They stand for two principles that God keeps driving home. First, if a man has been born of God he will hate sin and false teaching. Second, if a man has been born again he will love righteousness and truth. These two themes underlie every address to the unconverted; they are assumed in every exhortation to Christians. Paul put it this way:

> From the beginning God chose you to be saved *through the sanctifying work of the Spirit and through belief in the truth*. (*2 Thessalonians 2:13*)

Let us look at these two principles one at a time. The 'sanctification of the Spirit' that Paul speaks of means a separation by God's Spirit for God's use. When any object in the Old Testament was set apart for sacred use, it was said to be 'sanctified'. That meant that from that time forth it would be devoted to God alone. A clay pot, for example, might have dozens of uses. But if it was 'sanctified', it was used for sacred purposes only.

God's men and women have been set apart, or sanctified, for God alone. They have been separated from other men and women who serve other gods. Like the pot in my illustration, they did not set themselves apart. A divine person did it, namely, the Holy Spirit. Our salvation, as Paul says, comes 'through the sanctifying work of the Spirit.' We are made Christians by the Spirit of God.

When the Lord sets us apart for Himself He gives us new hearts. Each new heart hates sin. As a result, the believer now lives a life of repentance. The sin we once loved is now repulsive to us. We hate it, not merely because it injures us, but more importantly because it offends God. We are not yet completely free from sin. We sin too often. But we no longer find delight in sin. It is a burden to us. We know why the whole creation groans over sin, and we long for the hour when we shall never again offend our Lord!

Our new hearts also lead us to hate false teaching. Not that we are infallible! Sometimes we do not know whether this or that attractive doctrine is true. But when it is clear from God's Word that we are hearing or reading false-hood, we hate it. We say with Paul, 'Let God be true, and every man a liar' (*Romans 3:4*). His truth is more precious than all else to the Christian. We understand why Peter and Paul and the others died for the truth. They loved it because they loved God. They would not save their own lives and cast a shadow of doubt on His Word. Better to be crucified!

So the Christian is saved by believing and loving God's truth. That truth is not simply a bundle of unrelated facts. It is the gospel, a body of truths that centre upon Jesus Christ, who said of Himself, 'I am . . . the truth' (*John 14:6*). The Christian believes in, and loves, Jesus Christ. If a man does not trust and love the Lord Jesus, that man is not a Christian.

Many Christians shrink back from the question, 'Am *I* really converted? Do *I* truly believe in Jesus Christ?' They have been taught that thoughts like these are temptations, the next thing to unbelief. After all, did not God give them their assurance? What right do they have, then, to question God? In our anxiety to calm the doubts of believers we have often left the impression that it is wrong for one of God's people to question his own salvation. But is it wrong? Not according to the Scriptures!

In writing his second letter Peter gives a list of qualities that ought to belong to believers in Christ. He starts by exhorting his readers to 'make every effort to add to your faith goodness; and to goodness, knowledge,' and he continues through the list until he ends with 'love'. With these qualities still in mind, Peter adds this:

Therefore, my brothers, be all the more eager to make your calling and election sure. For if you do these things, you will never fall, and you will receive a rich welcome into the eternal kingdom of our Lord and Saviour Jesus Christ. (*2 Peter 1:10–12*)

Note especially these words: 'Be . . . eager to make your calling and election sure.'

In some ways this is a puzzling piece of advice. The 'calling' and the 'election' of any Christian are entirely the work of God. We did not call ourselves to Christ. It was God who called us at some point in our lives. And we surely did not elect ourselves to be Christians. Our election was a decision by God in eternity past. No amount of 'doing' on our part could make God either call us or elect us. He has already done those things, the whole matter is out of our hands.

Peter is not telling us in this passage how to become Christians. He does not believe that there is a way in which we may force God to elect us and call us. That is the farthest thing from Peter's mind. Instead he is doing something quite different. He is telling us that there is a way to confirm *to ourselves* that we belong to Christ. We might translate, 'Render your calling and election certain to yourselves.' Since calling and election are acts of God I cannot make them happen. But there is something I can do. I can check to see if they have been applied to me. I can find out whether my conviction that I belong to Christ is sound or whether it is a delusion. And Peter is telling me that that is what I had better do!

How can I be sure that I have been called by God? How can I know that I am one of God's elect? Not simply by asking whether I have 'made a decision.' Other men have 'made a decision' and have been lost. Not by asking whether I have been baptised. Multitudes that have been baptised will be in hell. No! that is not the way. Instead I must apply the tests that God gives me in His Word. (Look back at pp. 30ff.)

It is not hard to see what Peter expects us to do. He tells us to strive after a godly life. He exhorts us to 'make every effort' to add to our lives the qualities he lists, things like goodness and love. If we make some progress in that direction it will be evidence that God is already at work in us 'to will and to act according to his good purpose' (*Philippians 2:13*). It will show that we are indeed believers in Christ.

Does this mean that we are saved by our works? Not at all! What I am talking about is the evidence that we have been redeemed and that we have been born again. My works can add nothing to Christ's redemption. Neither can yours. And we cannot add anything to our new birth. It is an accomplished fact or it is not. But we can look for the signs that the Spirit has given us life. And those signs include a hunger and thirst for a godly life.

'Whoever has my commands and obeys them,' said Jesus, 'he is the one who loves me' (*John 14:21*). And again: 'If anyone loves me, he will obey my teaching . . . He who does not love me will not obey my teaching' (*John 14:23–24*). Is it the aim of my life to please Him? Or do I aim only to please myself? Do I hate sin and love righteousness? Do I hate sin for God's sake, because it offends Him, or do I hate it simply because it winds up hurting me and my loved ones? Do I love righteousness because it pleases God, or do I love it because it is 'the best policy', because it works out best for me? These are the Lord's tests and they are pointed. But they are more useful than merely remembering a day when I 'made a decision' for Christ.

These words of Christ also bring home the truth that there is a stark contrast between the true believer and the man of the world. If we hide that contrast from ourselves we may regret it for ever. Better to face it now, before it is too late. Do we dare fool ourselves? Better to tremble at the sight of hell, than to smile ourselves into a Christless grave.

Let me put this another way. Salvation is a free gift from God. God forbid that I should deny that! But salvation takes a certain form. God has described that form in His Word, so that we may see if it is going on within us. Paul, for example, ties together the gift and the form in writing to the church at Ephesus. First he speaks of God's free gift:

> For it is by grace you have been saved, through faith – and this not from yourselves, it is the gift of God – not by works, so that no-one can boast. (*Ephesians 2:8–9*)

What could be more free than this – 'a gift . . . not by works'?

But listen to Paul as he goes on:

> For we are God's workmanship, created in Christ Jesus to do good works, which God prepared in advance for us to do. (*Ephesians 2:10*)

Do you see what Paul says here? He tells us that God points a man in a special direction, toward 'good works', when He saves him. It is not right to credit salvation to good works. It is right and necessary, however, to expect good works to follow salvation. Salvation is not the result of good works, but good works *are* the result of salvation.

Some years ago I was sitting in a church building talking with a young lady who had gone deeply into sin. We will call her 'Mary'. 'Mary,' I said, 'why don't you stop your sin and begin to live for Christ?' She startled me with her answer. 'I know the gospel as well as you do,' she said. 'It's "Believe on the Lord Jesus Christ and thou shalt be saved." I believe, and I'm saved, and that's that!'

At the time I did not know how to answer Mary. I had watched her profess to come to Christ through a youth ministry in which I was active. She led a Bible club in her school; she gave a hearty testimony. Surely Mary was a Christian. If she was content to live the way she did, at least she would make it to heaven. At least that is what she thought, and I am ashamed to say that I did not know how to answer her.

But the answer is clear in Scripture even if I did not see it at the time. I wish I had been wise enough to say: 'Wait, Mary. How do you know that you are a believer? Is there the fruit of the Spirit in your life? You are right, Mary. We are to believe in Christ to be saved, in Christ and in Him alone. But do you really trust Christ to save you from *sin*? Are you trusting Him to clean up your life, or do you only care for getting to heaven? If that is all that interests you, Mary, you are not trusting Christ at all.'

Does that seem harsh? Let me tell you why it is true. *If I trust in Christ, I believe in the wisdom of His commands as well as in the sincerity of His promises*. God does not command me to believe in this or that promise of Christ. No, He tells me I must believe in the Lord Jesus Himself. If you are truly trusting Christ you will be convinced that His commands are wiser than your own inclinations. If that is not the case, you may be trusting a promise, but you are not trusting Jesus Christ, the One who made the promise.

Do I make it impossible for you to be sure that you belong to Christ? Are you saying, 'He does not want me to make sure of my standing with God, he wants to keep me in doubt'? Not at all! I want you to test yourself as gold is tested. But, most of all, I want you to come out unharmed.

You know why men test gold, why they put it in the fire. *They know that if it is gold, fire will not hurt it*. Men do not seek to destroy gold with fire. They do not seek to harm it in any way. Instead, they try to prove beyond all doubt that it is gold. And that is what God is doing when He applies the yardstick of His Word to His people. He seeks to show them, and the world, that *they are true Christians*.

In the process of proving gold to be true, impurities are burned away. Through the process of applying God's Word to our lives, the same thing will happen to the child of God. When we look in the mirror of Scripture we cannot be satisfied with ourselves. We are sure to see much that keeps the 'gold' from shining through. What will a genuine believer do in that case? He will determine, by the grace of God, to fight the impurities. That does not mean that he will be one hundred-per-cent successful. He will not! But if he has been born of God, his new heart will assert itself. It will move him in the right direction. The work of God will show in his life.

This test is really not so difficult to apply. It comes down to this: do you want God's way in your life, and do you trust Him to work His way in you? Does that sound hard? Let me help you further. A man who trusts God and Christ, trusts them with his circumstances. Ask yourself this: 'Do I want what God wants, even when I do not know what it is? Or must I know what His will is first, so that I can then decide whether I want it or not?' If you can say without hesitation, 'I want His will regardless of what it is!' you may be fooling yourself. But if you can say, despite much hesitation and reflection, 'Yes, I may be afraid, but I want Him to go ahead in spite of my fears', that is a good sign. If, the longer you reflect on it, the surer you are that God's way – whether poverty or riches, sickness or health – is the best way, the only way, then I do not fear for you. Any man can answer the question of God's will hastily with a resounding 'Yes!' But the Christian, with fear of his own weakness and failure, can do so after reflection on what it may mean. He can do so, because he trusts in God.

Here is Paul's advice to the Corinthian church and to you and me:

> Examine yourselves to see whether you are in the faith; test yourselves. Do you not realise that Christ Jesus is in you – unless, of course, you fail the test? (*2 Corinthians 13:5*)

What do you suppose Paul thought the outcome of this admonition would be? I have no doubt that he expected the Corinthians to come through the fire shining. Not all of them, of course! He hoped to awaken some who were deceived about their salvation. I hope to do that too.

But many of these men were Paul's converts. He had been thorough with them when he first met them. Paul could not read their hearts; only God could do that. But he rejoiced in them, as is made clear a few verses later when he writes:

> Finally, brothers, good-bye. Aim for perfection, listen to my appeal, be of one mind, live in peace. And the God of love and peace will be with you. (*2 Corinthians 13:11*)

Paul brought the Corinthians the warnings of the Lord, but he brought them hope as well.

Let me close this chapter in the same way. I have given you the warning to make sure of your standing with God. I have told you that this is necessary, not optional. I have told you the truth. But now let me point out something else. Let me give you hope. The Lord Jesus said, 'Come to me, all you who are weary and burdened, and I will give you rest' (*Matthew 11:28*). His invitation was genuine, sincere, unfeigned. Then He also said, 'Whoever comes to me I will never drive away' (*John 6:37*). You may trust Him to keep His word. You may cast the whole weight of your salvation on Him. You are authorised to do so. That is the point of His gracious words. If you truly believe in Christ, you shall not be put to shame, not even at the judgment bar of God. That is comfort, the hope, of every believer. It belongs to me; it belongs to you.

Christian: take heart!

Appendix: *Does 1 John 3:6 Teach the Security of Christians?*

1 John 3:6 says:

> No one who lives in him keeps on sinning. No one who continues to sin has either seen him or known him.

On the face of it this verse divides mankind into two classes. There are those who continue in sin and those who live in Christ. Each class, of course, excludes the other, and there is no third category. There are none who once knew Christ, but now are habitual sinners. The second phrase rules that out. Such a man has not 'either seen him or known him.'

But some have objected that the Greek text of that second phrase does not mean what it plainly implies in English. Here is an older example of this approach:

> It is no unusual thing with this apostle, both in his gospel and in his epistles, to put occasionally the *past* for the *present*, and the *present* for the *past* tense. It is very likely that here he puts after the manner of the Hebrew, the *preterite* for the *present*. He who sins against God *doth not see him, neither doth he know him*. The eye of his faith is darkened, so that he cannot see him as he formerly did; and he has no longer the experimental *knowledge* of God as his Father and Portion.

This statement is taken from the commentary of the Methodist preacher and theologian, Adam Clarke, who began publishing his comments on the whole Bible in

1810. He says expressly that he wrote 'not for the learned, but for comparatively simple people.' His aim accounts for his not giving us examples of other places where he thought John had exchanged the present tense for the past, or the past for the present. He is not to be faulted for this, but it makes it impossible for us to test his thesis. What we can say is this: more recent commentators, including those who do not believe that Christians are eternally secure, have not put their argument in just this way. It seems likely, then, that scholars no longer think that this is the explanation of John's use of the Greek perfect tense in 1 John 3:6.

Among commentators on the epistles of John during the last century, no name stands higher than that of Brooke Foss Westcott. After discussing 1 John 3:6 in some detail, he adds:

> The statement leaves on one side the question of the indefectibility of grace. It deals with the actual state of the man. Past sight and past knowledge cease to be unless they go forward.

In other words, in Westcott's view, 1 John 3:6 says nothing about whether a true believer may fall from grace (though his last sentence gives his own judgment on that question).

Several things need to be said about Westcott's statement. First, these words have the appearance of being an afterthought on Westcott's part. They are hard to square with this earlier comment on the same verse:

> Instead of saying 'every one that sinneth abideth not in (is cut off from) Him,' he substitutes a predicative clause which carries back the mind of the reader to an earlier stage of the fatal failure, as if he would say: 'In such a case there is no question of "abiding." The conditions of fellowship have never been satisfied. Such

a one hath not seen Christ (God in Christ) nor yet come to know Him.'[1]

On this understanding the verse would mean: 'No one who sins has *ever* satisfied the conditions of fellowship; no one who sins has *yet* come to know the Lord Jesus.' That, in turn, would be a plain statement of the security of every true Christian. Here, then, Westcott teaches 'the indefectibility of grace.' I do not mean, of course, that he actually held to the indefectibility of grace, but that his exposition of this portion of the verse necessarily demands it.

Second, if in fact this verse 'leaves on one side the question of the indefectibility of grace' then Westcott's statement that 'Past sight and past knowledge cease to be unless they go forward' is also not taught here. If 1 John 3:6 taught *that*, then past grace could be lost. Westcott, of course, had every right to make this theological judgment, but the reader must not take it as part of the exegesis of this verse.

Third, Westcott's comments on the word 'seen' show that he understood John's statement to concern more than 'the actual [i.e., the present] state of the man.' Referring to the Greek word for 'seen' he writes:

> The use of the word here in connexion with Christ seems to point to some teachers who appealed to their personal sight of the Lord (comp. i. 1ff.; John xix. 35, xx. 29) as giving authority to their false doctrine. Of such in spite of outward intercourse it could be said that 'they had not seen Christ' (comp. 2 Cor. v. 16).

It is not necessary for us to determine whether Westcott's reconstruction of the situation that called forth John's

---

[1] All the quotations from Westcott are taken from Brooke Foss Westcott, *The Epistles of St John*, Marcham Press, Appleford, Abingdon, 1966, p. 104.

statement is correct. What we are concerned with here is what Westcott thought, not whether he was right. He appears to mean the following: John knew of men who said, 'You must listen to us because we have seen the Lord Jesus.' But John could tell by their lives and teaching that they had not truly seen the Lord. Perhaps they had seen Him with their eyes, but they had only seen Him in a fleshly, carnal way. When they had looked at the Lord Jesus, they had not 'seen' Him, as He really was, at all.

Was this Westcott's understanding of the situation he describes? The evidence shows that it is. He speaks of 'personal sight' by these false teachers, and the references he uses to illustrate what he means are references to physical sight, either primarily (*John 19:35; 1 John 1:1ff.*) or exclusively (*John 20:29*). Then he says that this was 'outward intercourse,' plainly implying the need for inward intercourse. He concludes by saying that such teachers had not seen Christ. In what sense? 2 Corinthians 5:16 supplies his answer. There Paul wrote, 'So from now on we regard no one from a worldly point of view. Though we once regarded Christ in this way, we do so no longer.' That shows that inward 'sight' or understanding is what Westcott has in mind. When was it, that they had not 'seen' Christ? It was in the past, when they had looked at Him while He was in the flesh.[2] Further, up to the day John wrote, they still had not 'seen' Him.

In summary we may say that on Westcott's own showing, (1) John does deal with the indefectibility of grace and affirms it, and (2) John is reflecting on the past state of the men he describes and not simply on their 'actual' or present state.

I want to look next at two interpreters who have more

---

[2]Commentators are divided on whether Paul means that he had seen Jesus in the flesh or is simply speaking of how he had thought of Him, but that would not affect Westcott's argument.

recently taken up I John 3:6 with a view to denying the absolute security of all who are in Christ. Both Robert Shank and I. Howard Marshall have written comprehensive books on this theme. In addition Mr Marshall has written a well-received commentary on the Epistles of John. Let me take up Mr Shank's work first.[3]

Shank's argument, as we shall see, turns on the force of the perfect tense in Greek. Here are his words:

> Those who cite I John 3:6b as evidence that all 'Christians' whose lives contradict their profession necessarily are men who have never known Christ in a true saving relationship rest their argument, of course, on the English translation. But the English perfect is by no means the equivalent of the Greek perfect tense (*heōraken* and *egnōken*). The English perfect has but a single aspect, whereas the Greek perfect possesses two aspects. It is concerned, not only with the fact of an act in the past, but also with the fact that the results of that act continue to exist at the present moment. An act in the past, when considered entirely apart from the question of the continued existence of the results of that act, as of the moment of speaking, is affirmed by either the aorist or the imperfect. An expanded rendering of John's words is, 'whoever deliberately practises sin has not seen Him and continued seeing Him, nor known Him and continued knowing Him.' John's statement is applicable to men whose professions of faith have been false from the beginning, and it is equally applicable to apostates who have departed from true saving faith in Christ. (p. 98)

At this point Shank introduces a footnote and some references to B. F. Westcott and J. P. Lange. We will look at these shortly. He then gives us his conclusion:

[3]Robert Shank, *Life In The Son*, 2nd Edition, Westcott Publishers, Springfield, Missouri, 1977, pp. 98–99.

There is nothing about 1 John 3:6b that affirms that 'Christians' whose lives contradict their profession of faith are necessarily men who have never known Christ in a true saving relationship. (p. 99)

Two points in Shank's discussion call for comment. The first is a small matter, but is nevertheless worth noting. When he says that those who do not understand 1 John 3:6 as he does 'rest their argument, of course, on the English translation', his 'of course' is purely gratuitous and tends to prejudice the case in his favour. The suggestion is that it has never occurred to any Greek scholar to argue the security of Christians from 1 John 3:6b. But Shank is far too good a scholar himself, and too widely read, seriously to hold that opinion.[4]

The heart of Shank's argument turns on his understanding of the force of the perfect tense in Greek. He

[4]Representative commentators, competent in the Greek language, who have held that 1 John 3:6b teaches the security of the Christian include John Cotton (17th Cent.), John Gill (18th Cent.), Alfred Plummer (19th Cent.), and John R. W. Stott (20th Cent.). The reader may consult the commentaries by each of these men at 1 John 3:6. Those not familiar with his commentary may be surprised to find Alfred Plummer included among them. For that reason I want to quote his comment at length. It is taken from *The Cambridge Bible for Schools and Colleges, The Epistles of S. John,* Cambridge, 1885, p. 125:

'No one who sins has seen Christ or attained to a knowledge of Him. What does S. John mean by this strong statement? It will be observed that it is the antithesis of the preceding statement; but, as usual, instead of giving us the simple antithesis, "Every one that sinneth abideth not in Him", he expands and strengthens it into "Every one that sinneth hath not seen Him, neither come to know Him". S. John does not say this of every one who commits a sin, but of the habitual sinner (present participle). Although the believer sometimes sins, yet not sin, but opposition to sin, is the ruling principle of his life; for whenever he sins he confesses it, and wins forgiveness, and perseveres with his self-purification.

But the habitual sinner does none of these things: sin is his ruling principle. And this could not be the case if he had ever really known Christ. Just as apostates by leaving the Church prove that they have never really belonged to it (ii. 19), so the sinner by continuing in sin proves that he has never really known Christ.'

makes three points that are important to our understanding of 1 John 3:6.

1. The English perfect tense does not exactly correspond to the Greek perfect tense ('by no means' is again gratuitous).

2. The Greek perfect tense not only looks backward to a past act, but also assumes that the past act's results continue.

3. An accurate rendering – and Shank suggests one – will show that no future security for Christians is implied in John's statement.

Let us examine these three points. Shank's first point is correct, though, as I have suggested by my parenthetical remark, somewhat overstated. Robert W. Funk has written more accurately, '. . . the perfect tenses are used in a slightly different way in Greek. The difference is not large but it is now and then puzzling.'[5] Shank's second point, that the perfect tense looks at both a past act and its present effect is also true and will become important in our further discussion.

It is Shank's third point that needs to be questioned. Is his suggested rendering of 1 John 3:6b accurate? Let me quote it once more:

> Whoever deliberately practises sin has not seen Him and continued seeing Him, nor known Him and continued knowing Him.

The point of this rendering, evidently, is to place the emphasis on the words 'and continued' in each of the phrases. If these men ever saw Christ they have not *continued* to see Him; if they once knew Christ they have not *continued* to know Him. Shank's point will be, then, that nothing at all is asserted about the sinner's past condition. We cannot tell from 1 John 3:6 whether the

[5]Robert W. Funk, *A Beginning-Intermediate Grammar Of Hellenistic Greek*, 2nd Edition, Scholars Press, Missoula. Montana, n.d., p. 627.

sinner once knew Christ or not. In other words, the perfect tense here functions precisely as the present tense would. An equally valid translation would then be: 'Whoever deliberately practises sin does not see Him or know Him.'

As it happens, if the Greek word for 'know' stood here alone there might be some force in Shank's contention. Some think that John uses the perfect tense of *ginōskō* as if it were a present tense.[6] But even this is doubtful. There is a Greek word for 'know', *oida*, which functions as a present tense although it is a perfect in form. K. L. McKay has written on the distinction between the two. He says: 'As a perfect, *oida* is remarkable in that, although it is one of the most commonly used perfects, it rarely, if ever, conveys any clear implication of the action by which its state (of knowledge) was established . . . While in many respects very similar to *oida*, *egnōka*, the perfect of *ginōskō*, normally seems to differ in having an inbuilt reference to the event of acquisition of knowledge.'[7] If we adopt this understanding of *ginōskō* we would translate 'No one who practises sin has seen Him or has come to know Him.' Once again we would have a reference to *both* the present and the past, but this translation would negate both aspects, so that it would be clear that the person spoken of had *never* known Christ.[8] The burden of proof is

---

[6]To help the reader make a judgment on this, here are the places I have found where John uses the perfect tense of *ginōskō*: John 5:42; 6:69; 8:52; 8:55; 14:7,9; 17:7. 1 John 2:3,4,13a,13c [14a in UBS Greek NT],14; 3:6,16; 4:16. 2 John 1. Both the NASB and the fifth edition of Weymouth's version support the present meaning for *ginōskō* in 1 John 3:6. Both read: 'No one who sins has seen Him or knows Him'. NASB has 'has known' as an alternate reading in the margin.

[7]K. L. McKay, 'ON THE PERFECT AND OTHER ASPECTS IN NEW TESTAMENT GREEK', *Novum Testamentum*, XXIII, 4 (1981), p. 299.

[8]In fact, it is precisely this understanding of the perfect tense of *ginōskō* that is reflected in the NIV's translation of 1 John 2:3, 'We know that *we have come to know* him if we obey his commands.'

on Shank to show that *ginōskō* in 1 John 3:6 is to be treated as present in force. But even if that could be shown, the case is quite different with *heōraken*, the word commonly translated 'has seen'.

The most obvious way to show that 'has seen' is the preferred translation of *heōraken* is by consulting a large number of translations, especially the 'committee versions' where a number of Greek scholars have collaborated to produce the final form. The most widely used 'committee versions' in English include the KJV, Douay-Rheims (Challoner ed.), RV, ASV, RSV, NEB, NASB and the NIV. A quick check of these versions will show that *in every case* the translators have used the English perfect tense to translate the Greek verb. They have done this, no doubt, because they felt that the English perfect brought out the meaning of the verb better than an English present could do. But as we have seen, if Shank's understanding of the text were correct an English present would be more nearly accurate.

It is particularly impressive to note the way in which the RV, ASV, NEB and NASB treat this text. Each of these versions translates *ginōskō* by an English present tense and *heōraken* by an English perfect tense, *showing that the distinct nuances of the two tenses in English were clearly before the minds of the translators as they brought the text to its final form.*[9]

Another way to examine the soundness of Shank's approach is open to us. John has a particular fondness for the perfect tense. Morton Scott Enslin has counted 195 instances of the perfect tense in John's Gospel in 53 pages

[9]Other versions at hand show a unanimous preference for the English perfect tense for *heōraken*. These include both the translations made by men named Charles Williams, along with the Beck, Moffatt, Goodspeed, Phillips, Wuest and New King James versions. All of these except Wuest translate *both* verbs as perfects. Cf. also Martin Luther's German version.

of the Westcott and Hort text and 49 instances in 7 pages of the Epistle we are presently examining.[10] After comparing these figures with the instances of the perfect tense in the Synoptic Gospels Enslin concludes, 'John's fondness for the perfect is far above average.' We see, then, that there are sufficient examples for us to gather how John uses the perfect tense. More important for this study is the fact that there are 10 places in his Gospel and 6 places in his Epistles where John negates a perfect tense, using the Greek negative *ou* just as he uses it in 1 John 3:6b. An examination of these instances will show us whether John habitually negates only the present state that is implied by the perfect tense in Greek, or whether he also habitually negates the past action that results in the present state. These instances are in the following table:

TEXT	DISCUSSION
John 4:38	'what you have not worked for.' Here Jesus clearly excludes all prior activity of His disciples. I.e., He negates the past.
John 6:32	'It is not Moses who has given you the bread . . .' Jesus looks back to Moses, and negates the past.
John 6:46	'No-one has seen the Father' Ever! Past negated.
John 8:41	'We are not illegitimate children.' The NIV has chosen to paraphrase. But note Funk's treatment of this verse as demonstrating 'the characteristic nuance of the perfect (past act with

[10]Morton S. Enslin, 'THE PERFECT TENSE IN THE FOURTH GOSPEL', *Journal of Biblical Literature*, vol. LV, 1936, pp. 121–122. Actually Enslin found more than 195 perfects in John's Gospel. He explains the principles on which he excluded some from his count on page 121.

	effects reaching to the present).' He offers this translation: '*We were not illicitly conceived* (and so are not illegitimate)'.[11] The speakers negate the past.
John 8:55	'Though you do not know him'. The verb here is *ginōskō*. We may treat this instance as uncertain, but if we understand *ginōskō* as suggested by McKay above, then Jesus negates the past here also.
John 12:30	'This voice was for your benefit, not mine.' Here Jesus clearly negates the past.
John 14:9	'Don't you know me, Philip . . . ?' *Ginōsko*– again. See note on 8:55.
John 20:30	'miraculous signs . . . which are not recorded in this book.' Here the Greek word *gegraptai* is used, a word that some think has present force. Thus, this instance is doubtful.[12]
1 John 1:10	'If we claim we have not sinned . . .' Here John looks back and clearly negates the past.[13]
1 John 4:10	'. . . not that we loved God . . .' But to some degree we love God *now*. John negates the past.
1 John 4:18	'The man who fears is not made perfect in love.' The Greek verb translated 'made perfect' describes a state

[11]Robert W. Funk, op. cit., p. 630.

[12]Cf. E. D. Burton, *Syntax of the Moods and Tenses in New Testament Greek*, Edinburgh, 1898, p. 37 where Burton cites *gegraptai* as one of 'a few verbs which use the Perfect in this [present] sense only.'

[13]Incidentally, this is the only instance in the NT of *hamartanō* in the perfect tense.

	by definition. This instance is doubt-ful.
1 John 4:20	'God . . . whom he has not seen.' Visual sight is under discussion. Cf. 4:12. Here John negates the past.
1 John 5:10	'. . . he has not believed the testimony that God has given about his Son.' Once again we have a word that Burton takes to be present in meaning.[14] This instance must be treated as doubtful.

(I have omitted from the table 1 John 3:6b, the text under discussion, and 3 John 11 which is parallel to it. I have also omitted John 7:19 and 10:34 where *ou* with the perfect is a sign of a question, not a genuine negation.)

The preceding table shows the following:

1. It is not possible to be certain about every instance of John's negating a perfect, since some of them involve forms which may have come to be used in the present sense over the centuries of Greek usage.
2. John normally has in mind not only the present but also the past when he negates a word in the perfect tense.
3. There is no clear instance where John undoubtedly uses a Greek verb that has both a perfect sense and a perfect form to indicate results without reference to the past action that produced those results.

The conclusion to be drawn from this portion of our study is as follows: Shank is totally unwarranted in pleading for his understanding of 1 John 3:6b *on the basis of the difference between the English and Greek perfect tenses*. What he needed to do, and has not done, is to show that, contrary to John's usual practice, in 1 John 3:6b John has negated the perfect tense of *horao* with a different intention than he usually

[14]E. D. Burton, op. cit., p. 38.

displays. For clearly, in negating the perfect tense of a verb, John's normal intent is to negate the past as well as the present.

Before we leave Shank, however, we want to look at the footnote and the references to B. F. Westcott and J. P. Lange to which I referred on page 158. No discussion of Westcott is necessary since all that Shank does is cite the quotation from Westcott with which I have already dealt. From J. P. Lange's Commentary he cites the following: 'John's idea therefore is this: Every one that sinneth, and that while he is sinning, is one in whom seeing and knowing Christ is a fact of the past, but without continuing to act and to last to the present.'[15] As Shank points out, this translation makes John speak of apostasy, since it asserts 'seeing and knowing Christ' as 'a fact of the past.'

A few comments are in order:

1. This understanding precludes any reference to 'men whose professions of faith have been false from the beginning,' a group that Shank's understanding necessarily includes. (The quotation is from Shank's own words quoted above.) Braune thinks John is speaking of genuine believers who have fallen away; Shank thinks that is an open question. Beyond that Braune says explicitly, 'It is wholly unwarranted to take the Perfect in the sense of the Present.' Yet that is what Shank feels must be done. It is evident then that Braune does not support Shank's understanding of the text and, hence, cannot be called in as a witness for it.

2. Braune's understanding that the text speaks of just one class of sinners (apostates), however, is even less likely

---

[15]The reference is taken from Karl Braune, 'THE EPISTLES GENERAL OF JOHN', in John Peter Lange, *Commentary on the Holy Scriptures*, reprint Zondervan, Grand Rapids, 1960, vol IX, *in loc*. [This is page 102 in the commentary on 1 John, but the numbering starts anew for each commentary within the volume.]

than Shank's. The text occurs in a passage that is a sustained comparison between the only two kinds of men that live in the world, those who are 'of the devil' and those who 'are born of God.' To introduce a distinction within the former class is to complicate the passage unnecessarily.

3. Hence the quotation from Braune in Lange's Commentary adds nothing to Shank's argument. In fact, if Braune's understanding were correct it would refute Shank's position! Evidently, then, it is added only because Braune disbelieves in the full security of Christians.

Finally, let us look at Shank's footnote, that I have referred to above. The portion we want to examine reads:

> Many have appealed to Matt. 7:23 to contend that all false prophets (*vv. 15ff*) and imposters are men whom Christ has never known, according to His statement, 'I never knew you.' Let us observe that Jesus declared only that He would *profess* to them (*homolegeō*) that He never knew them. Cf. Luke 13:25,27, where Jesus warned His hearers that He would say of them, 'I know you not whence ye are' – which obviously could be true only figuratively, rather than literally (*cf. John 8:23,44*).

The reason for this footnote is clear. It is to show that another verse often thought to teach the security of Christians, *in terms very similar to 1 John 3:6b*, does not teach what it might first be taken to mean. Shank's proof for this position is twofold. Let's look at it more closely.

The words of Christ, 'I never knew you,' certainly seem to teach that those that He rejects were never savingly related to Him. But Shank points out that 'Jesus declared only that He would *profess* to them (*homolegeō*) that He never knew them.' I am unable to see how Jesus' choice of the word *homolegeō* makes any difference here. The Greek word means to 'confess' or 'declare' something. It is equivalent to Jesus saying, 'This is what I will declare to men at the judgment: I never knew you.' It is hard to see how this changes the meaning of Jesus' statement.

It is likely, however, that Shank did not intend this argument to stand alone as a proof, but to be taken with what follows. In that case he may mean, 'Jesus did indeed profess that he would use these words to those that he rejects. But we can see, by comparing them with the words in Luke 13, that he did not mean them to be taken literally. And, as Shank says, the words 'I know you not whence ye are,' if spoken by Christ at the judgment 'could be true only figuratively.' At the judgment Christ will know all things about all men.

It seems to me that Shank has missed an important distinction between these two texts. The Matthew 7 passage contains a plain statement about the future judgment. Though there are parables on both sides of it, the paragraph 7:21–23 is not in parabolic form. It contains a direct statement about what Jesus will say in that day: 'I never knew you.' But the passage in Luke 13 has strong parabolic or figurative elements woven into it. We may see this by setting Luke 13:22–27 before us:

> Then Jesus went through the towns and villages, teaching as he made his way to Jerusalem. Someone asked him, 'Lord, are only a few people going to be saved?'
>
> He said to them, 'Make every effort to enter through the narrow door, because many, I tell you, will try to enter and will not be able to. Once the owner of the house gets up and closes the door, you will stand outside knocking and pleading, "Sir, open the door for us."
>
> 'But he will answer, "I don't know you or where you come from."
>
> 'Then you will say, "We ate and drank with you, and you taught in our streets."

'But he will reply, "I don't know you or where you come from. Away from me, all you evildoers!"'

As Creed has noted, 'The connexion between *v.* 24 and *v.* 25 depends upon the parabolic use of "the door".'[16] Jesus uses the word 'door' figuratively the first time He uses it. Then he extends the figure, placing the door into a house and speaking of 'the owner of the house.' In so doing he creates a small parable of the judgment. The owner of the house is not Jesus, but he represents Jesus. Hence Jesus speaks of him in the third person – 'he will answer' and 'he will reply'. It is the owner of the house, with all the human limitations we often find in parabolic characters, who says these words. That means they are part of the incidental details of the story and not an exact representaton of the judgment day. As Shank has told us, we cannot take these words literally.[17] But the words of Matthew 7:23, in contrast to these in Luke, stand as the words of Christ Himself, representing His mind in a matter of supreme importance, the issue of the security of the regenerate. Matthew 7:23 teaches the same truth as 1 John 3:6: no true believer will ever be lost.

Finally I want to look at the contributions of I. Howard Marshall to this subject of the force of 1 John 3:6. As noted earlier, Marshall has written a book on the security of the Christian, as well as a commentary on 1 John.[18] His

---

[16]John Martin Creed, *The Gospel According to St. Luke*, MacMillan & Co., London, 1965, p. 184.

[17]There are many of Jesus' parables with characters that represent God or Christ. In a number of these the characters say things that neither God or Christ would say. Cf. for example, Luke 16:8; 19:22; 20:13.

[18]The book is: I. Howard Marshall, *Kept By The Power of God*, Bethany Fellowship, Minneapolis, 1975. The commentary is in the NIC series: I. Howard Marshall, *The Epistles of John*, Eerdmans, Grand Rapids, 1978. Hereafter I will refer to the book as *Kept*, and the commentary as *NIC*.

general conclusion on the subject is to treat apostasy as possible, but as a relatively rare occurrence.[19]

In *Kept* Marshall treats the Epistles of John as a unit (pp. 186–190) and looks at 1 John 3:6–10 under the heading 'Sin and Perseverance.' Here he assumes the understanding of 1 John 3:6b that I have been contending for throughout this chapter. He says, for example, 'The experience of being born of God and thus receiving the divine nature is said to make the believer sinless; he does not and cannot sin. The person who sins does not know Christ (*1 John 3:6–10; 5:18*)' (p. 187). If we turn to *NIC* we find the same understanding, this time with an explicit reference to the force of the perfect tense. On 'seeing' Christ, Marshall says:

> Clearly, 'seeing' with the eyes is not meant. John is thinking rather of 'seeing' the significance of Jesus as the one who reveals the unseen God. *The perfect tense of the verb will then denote the initial act of conversion which leads on to a continuing experience.* [Italics added]. John's point is that nobody can go through such an experience and remain capable of sinning. (pp. 183–184)

Here are the central points I have been making throughout this chapter. (1) The perfect tense does contain a reference to the past 'sight' of Christ as well as the present results of that sight. (2) 1 John 3:6b negates both the past and present, i.e., it denies that anyone 'sinning' has ever seen or known Christ. That is the true force of the perfect tense in this passage. Most significantly, what we have

---

[19]Cf. this statement on the 'sin that leads to death' in 1 John from *Kept*, p. 190: 'It must be most strongly emphasized that such a serious sin is spoken of only as a possibility and indeed as a rare possibility. It is not the normal issue of the Christian life. That life is essentially one in which the believer abides in Christ and does not, yea cannot, sin as a result of the power for victory which God gives to those who are born of Him.' This quotation is rather John's conclusion as Marshall sees it, but since Marshall holds a high view of Scripture I take it that it represents his own view as well.

here is the understanding of a competent, 'hostile' witness.[20]

Earlier I told you that Marshall is opposed to the idea of the absolute security of the regenerate. The above quotations seem to say otherwise, and that leads us to the heart of Marshall's understanding of the passage in which 1 John 3:6 occurs. Though he makes the statements quoted above in all seriousness, nevertheless he does not think that they settle the question of whether a man who was once saved can ever be lost. But how can this be?

Here is Marshall's own answer:

> . . . what John is depicting here is the ideal character of the Christian. The simplest form of this view is that the verse depicts what ought to be the character of the Christian. The saying is to be 'explained on the analogy of (the Apostle's) way of speaking throughout the Epistle of the ideal reality of the life of God and the life of sin as absolutely excluding one another,' says Alford . . . Another, complementary way of regarding John's statements is to see them as implicit imperatives. They are statements of what Christians ought to be, and are thus injunctions to them to approach the ideal. (*NIC*, pp. 180–181)

If this seems to be an odd way to look at John's direct statements, Marshall has his reasons. There is, of course, his conviction derived from his understanding of other texts in the New Testament that absolute security is not the teaching of the Scriptures. How far that conviction affects his reading of the present passage, it is, of course, impossible to say. We do know one thing that looms very large in his understanding. Marshall finds it difficult to be

---

[20]I dislike the word 'hostile' in this connection, but it is in keeping with common usage and the reader will understand that it is not intended as a reflection on Dr Marshall.

satisfied with any of the alternate ways of taking 1 John 3:6. He recognises that the 'ideal' view will not commend itself to every scholar,[21] but it seems the best of the possibilities. This, of course, is a reasonable way to proceed.

Why not, then, adopt the ideal view? The answer seems clear: 1 John in general, and this passage in particular, are concerned with empirically identifying those who belong to Christ, both to weed out (or conceivably, to correct) the false and to encourage the true believer. To introduce the 'ideal view' into this passage is to take an important step toward defeating the purpose of the book.

Let's first look at the book as a whole. One of the striking things about 1 John is its concern with the claims of men who profess in one way or another to know God. Note the following examples:

> If we claim to have fellowship with him yet walk in darkness, we lie and do not live by the truth. (*1:6*)
> If we claim to be without sin, we deceive ourselves and the truth is not in us. (*1:8*)
> If we claim we have not sinned, we make him out to be a liar and his word has no place in our lives. (*1:10*)
> The man who says, 'I know him,' but does not do what he commands is a liar, and the truth is not in him. (*2:4*)
> Whoever claims to live in him must walk as Jesus did. (*2:6*)[22]

[21]Cf. his statement: 'It would seem that this view [i.e., the "ideal view"] too is not without difficulty' (*NIC*, p. 181), and this acknowledgment concerning the view that the sin the Christian cannot do, is habitual, characteristic sin: 'This is perhaps the most popular understanding among British commentators. It has the merit of providing a view of the life of the believer which is consistent with New Testament teaching generally . . .' (*NIC*, p. 180).

[22]See also 2:9. In addition a large number of verses have to do with the weighing of claims where the words 'claim' and 'says' are not used. E.g., 2:5,10,11; 2:22,29; 3:18; 4:1–3, 6,20 etc. Cf. G. C. Berkouwer, *Man: The Image Of God*, Grand Rapids, 1962, p. 116.

It is important to see that the book of 1 John arose out of a concrete situation that demanded tangible yardsticks for measuring the reality of professions of faith. Certainly theology is taught here. But it is theology that can be taken into the marketplace; it is not at all abstract. It was intended to be applied to life situations, there and then. Whatever may be the merits of an 'ideal' representation of the Christian life in another context, it is not required here. Something far different is needed and that is what John has given.

What we find in the book as a whole is also evident in the passage before us. John's concern throughout 2:29 to 3:10 (and beyond) is practical.[23] Look, for example, at 3:1. God calls us His children, but is that concretely true or is it only an ideal representation? Here is John's answer: 'And that is what we are!' But most importantly look at verse 10:

> This is how we know who the children of God are and who the children of the devil are: Anyone who does not do what is right is not a child of God; neither is anyone who does not love his brother.

The point is this: there is a practical way to determine who is a child of God and who is not. But an ideal representation of the Christian life cannot supply such a criterion. Therefore John cannot be expounding an ideal view, for at best such a view could lead us to conclude that we are partly children of God and partly children of the devil. Though, of course, sin still clings in some measure to the Christian, no one could read 1 John and suppose that John

---

[23]To the objection that to set a perfect standard before Christians is immensely practical, it is sufficient to reply that it would not be practical for the end in view here. So far from being a help in identifying true and false professors, it would eliminate all men equally from the ranks of God's children.

means to set before us such a monstrosity as the true nature of a child of God.[24]

We have been asking the question: does 1 John 3:6 teach the security of believers? We are in a position to answer that question now. Here are the salient points:

1. John does indeed address the question of whether a man can fall from grace in 1 John 3:6. His use of the perfect tense in Greek shows that he has in view both the past action of 'seeing' Christ and the present result of that action when he says, 'No one who continues to sin has . . . seen him . . .'

2. A statement parallel to this one exists in the Gospel of Matthew 7:23. In it Jesus tells men who made impressive professions of faith, 'I never knew you.'

3. It is not possible to treat these statements as representing an 'ideal' view of Christians. The passage, and indeed the book, has for a main purpose laying before us the criteria for separating a true profession of 'knowing God' from a false one.[25] 1 John 3:6 is intended to further that purpose.

In the light of these points we may say without hesitation: Yes, 1 John 3:6 teaches that a believer in Jesus Christ can *never* be lost.

---

[24]It is no objection to this understanding of the text that it may be difficult to apply this criterion. The choice is between a criterion that is difficult to apply and one that is impossible to apply without concluding that there are no children of God in this world.

[25]The nature of the practical aim of the book also gives us a standpoint from which to evaluate Henry Alford's claim quoted by Marshall that John is 'speaking throughout the Epistle of the ideal reality of the life of God and the life of sin as absolutely excluding one another.' Whatever we may think of Alford's antithesis as a general truth, it is clear that it would not have met the practical interests addressed in 1 John.